EAST GERMAN PRODUCTIVITY AND THE TRANSITION TO THE MARKET ECONOMY

East German Productivity and the Transition to the Market Economy

Comparisons with west Germany and Northern Ireland

D.M.W.N. HITCHENS
Department of Economics
The Queen's University of Belfast

K. WAGNER
Technische Universität and Science Centre Berlin

J.E. BIRNIE
Department of Economics
The Queen's University of Belfast

Avebury

Aldershot · Brookfield USA · Hong Kong · Singapore · Sydney

Published by
Avebury
Ashgate Publishing Limited
Gower House
Croft Road
Aldershot
Hants GU11 3HR
England

Ashgate Publishing Company
Old Post Road
Brookfield
Vermont 05036
USA

Reprinted 1994

A CIP catalogue record for this book is available from the British Library

Library of Congress Cataloging-in-Publication Data
Hitchens, D. M. W. N.
    East German productivity and the transition to the market economy
    : comparisons with West Germany and Northern Ireland / D.M.W.N.
    Hitchens, K. Wagner, J.E. Birnie
        p.   cm.
    ISBN 1-85628-443-3 : $59.95
    1. Industrial productivity--Germany (East) 2. Industrial
    productivity--Germany (West) 3. Industrial productivity--Northern
    Ireland. I. Wagner, Karin. II. Birnie, J. E., 1965- III . Title.
    HC290.I52H58   1993
    338.9431--dc20   93-16352
                                                                 CIP
ISBN 1 85628 443 3

Printed and Bound in Great Britain by
Athenaeum Press Ltd, Newcastle upon Tyne

Contents

List of tables

Foreword

This book represents one of the first empirical studies of firms in a former communist bloc country. The authors have undertaken a comprehensive assessment of the efficiency and the competitiveness of a sample of east German plants shortly after the unification of Germany. They identify the problems encountered by firms in the transformation process where they must cope with the challenges caused by drastic changes in their markets and other aspects of their socio-economic environment.

A major strength of this study is that it is undertaken on a micro level. This enables the authors to take account of the heterogeneity among plants and to analyse a number of factors that are often neglected by other investigators most of whom concentrate on aggregate data for groups of plants or firms. Another substantial advantage of the approach taken is that they compare the results for east Germany to matched plants in west Germany and Northern Ireland. This introduces a degree of context into the analysis that cannot be achieved in studies that are limited to a single country or region. Moreover the international and inter-regional comparisons provide realistic benchmarks from which to draw policy conclusions.

The authors discuss policy options aimed at promoting competitiveness which are especially valuable given labour costs are rising towards parity with west Germany. The recommendations raise important questions for further research such as how to facilitate technology transfer, effective training programmes and inter-firm co-operation. The study shows that co-operation between eastern and western firms may be very helpful in stimulating productivity of lagging firms.

It would be desirable if economic development in east Germany could be monitored continuously using the method adopted in this study. This would yield insights into the process of economic convergence which would have wider application to problem regions throughout eastern and western Europe.

Professor Dr. Michael Fritsch
Bergakademie Frieberg and
Technische Universtät Berlin

Preface

Once the night-train from Köln to Berlin crossed the Elbe, I got no more sleep.

Chancellor Konrad Adenauer

Perhaps the single most important economic policy goal for east Germany is to promote the greatest possible convergence between living standards in east and west Germany in the shortest time possible. It is within this context that the basic aim of this book is to investigate the nature and extent of productivity convergence between samples of east and west German manufacturing firms since unification. Given the continuing adjustment process from planned economy to market system it was especially significant that this study was undertaken during an early phase (January 1991-January 1992) of German monetary and economic union.

During the initial euphoria of unification it was predicted that it would be straightforward to transplant to east Germany an economic miracle equivalent to that experienced in west Germany in the 1950s. Now the pendulum seems to have swung back too far in the direction of pessimism to the extent that it is forecast that convergence might take the best part of a century if indeed it ever occurs (Barro and Sala-i-Martin, 1991). Our own results provide grounds for more optimism. For example, the underlying productivity performance of sample firms included in this study jumped by 50 per cent during the first year of unification. By mid 1991 the east German sample firms had already attained levels of physical productivity (i.e. volume of output per head) equivalent to that of firms in a region of the United

Kingdom (though product quality was still lower than in the UK). In other words, the performance of the east German firms surveyed (e.g. in their capacity to obtain very large and quick productivity gains through removing previous X-inefficiency) indicates that the east German economy could surpass the "normal" rates of convergence displayed by capitalist economies or even the post-war economic miracles of western Europe and the Pacific Rim (Dornbusch and Wolf, 1992).

The special advantages enjoyed by east Germany (e.g. access to west German government funds and capital market) make it hazardous to draw wider lessons for other eastern European economies. Nevertheless, east Germany as a result of the very abrupt nature of monetary and economic union represents an accelerated version of the transition process which the other communist bloc economies are now experiencing. One finding of this study which can be generalised is that company survival will depend largely on the ability to produce goods which match western quality standards. Such product quality is in turn dependent most critically on the level of human capital (the up to dateness of physical capital may often be of lesser significance) and to the extent that some of the eastern European economies (e.g. Czechoslovakia and Hungary) share this advantage of an endowment of basic technical skills bodes well for the development process. The eastern European economies are however likely to find it harder to use those methods to supplement the skills base which east German firms have employed (e.g. importing west Germans to senior positions, sending east Germans on study courses in west Germany). Nevertheless, inward investment and joint ventures will be valuable to the extent that these promote "learning by seeing" on the part of indigenous companies in eastern Europe.

If the convergence process in manufacturing productivity levels is in large part propelled by human capital then our relative optimism about east Germany's prospects implies pessimism about the potential of those western European depressed regions which have poorer skills endowments than those of the former communist economy. The plants in east Germany were matched with counterparts in Northern Ireland, the latter being one of the western European regions which some commentators think east Germany is in danger of imitating (another being the Italian *Mezzogiorno*). The Northern Ireland economy, like its east German counterpart, is heavily dependent on public spending and on a large scale transfer of fiscal resources from the rest of the national economy. Moreover, several decades of intensive subsidisation of firms (and especially of capital equipment) appears to have weakened productivity performance and produced high levels of overmanning. Northern Ireland (and indeed, the Republic of Ireland also) are examples of regions which have failed over the long run (i.e. 70 years) to

xiv

achieve significant economic convergence even with the rest of the United Kingdom let alone western European best practice. East German manufacturing has better prospects given the good technical quality of the the labour force compared with a deficient stock of human capital in Ireland.

The authors wish to acknowledge the funding for this study by the European Commission, Directorate General for Regional Policy. The early process of planning the project was greatly facilitated by a grant provided by the British Council. We are also especially grateful to the part played by Jörn Mallok who acted as research assistant in Berlin and who was involved in both company visits and data analysis. He also helped the research team from his perspective as an east German graduate engineer providing additional technical knowledge. A study of this nature would have been impossible but for the co-operation of the firms involved. The managers were generous with their time even in those cases where their companies were in the midst of very stressful reorganisation.

Dr Clifford Jefferson (Head of the Department of Economics) and Professor John Spencer (Director of the School of Social Sciences) at Queen's University Belfast greatly facilitated us in the underlying research and production of this book. We were also assisted by helpful comments on the contents by Professor John Spencer. Professor Michael Fritsch who is a specialist in German regional economics and policy has very kindly written a foreword. The final production has been possible with painstaking assistance from Mary Trainor and Eileen Maguire and in matters of typesetting and layout we were greatly helped by the patient and helpful advice of Suzanne Evins of Avebury.

The usual disclaimer applies.

D.M.W.N.H.
K.W.
J.E.B.
1 November 1992

1 Comparative industrial productivity in east Germany: An overview

Introduction

Unification of East and West Germany (hereafter referred to as east and west Germany, with DDR sometimes used for pre-1989 east Germany) has presented an opportunity to investigate to what extent and by what means surviving east German companies will be able to raise their productivity (or output per head) to west German standards by 1994, when parity of wage levels is likely to occur.

This study was conducted with the intention of advising industrial policy making in east Germany, eastern Europe and peripheral regions within the EC. Thirty-two plants in east Germany were compared to 34 in west Germany and 39 in Northern Ireland and productivity benchmark estimates between east and west German sample firms have been established. These three samples were matched by product type and size of firm. At the time of interview 40 per cent of the east German firms sampled had already been privatised by the state holding agency, the *Treuhand*, and in 70 per cent of these cases purchased by west German companies.

Particular emphasis has been placed on the explanations for comparatively low productivity levels in east German firms and especially the importance of factors such as machinery and skills and training levels given that these factors had already been considered as explanations of the productivity gap between Northern Ireland, Britain and west Germany (Hitchens, Wagner and Birnie, 1990).

1

The comparative productivity record

Prior to German monetary unification on 1 July 1990 comparative productivity for the whole industrial sector (i.e. manufacturing plus mining, construction and utilities) has been estimated at about 50 per cent that of the level in west Germany (Korn, 1991). This is similar to the comparative productivity estimated for 1983 (*Deutschen Bundestag*, 1987). The productivity of the entire DDR economy in 1989/90 has been variously estimated at about 40 per cent of that achieved by west Germany (i.e. comparative GDP per employee as estimated by DIW, 1990a, 1990b; Filip-Koln and Ludwig, 1990; Schmieding, 1990; the potential unreliability of such comparisons is considered by Akerlof, Rose, Yellen and Hessenius, 1991).

Merkel and Wahl (1991) suggest that comparative GDP per employee has been in long run trend decline relative to west German levels since the 1950s and the relative position may have declined further in the first year since unification (the official statistics suggest that comparative GDP per employee fell from being 37.1 per cent of the level in west Germany in the second quarter of 1990 to 34.2 per cent in the second quarter of 1991 and 34.6 per cent in the first quarter of 1992; Financial Times, 1992, September 9; *Institut der Deutschen Wirtschaft*, 1992, August 13). At unification annual wage rates were 32 per cent of the west German level (using a conversion rate of 1 DM = 1 *Ost Mark*). The most up to date information from the German statistical authorities available at the time of writing suggest that in the last quarter of 1990 output per head in east German manufacturing was still less than a quarter that of manufacturing in west Germany while wages and salaries per capita were less than one-third those in the west.

A series of wage agreements had raised east German annual wage rates to an average of 43 per cent of the west German level by the first half of 1991. By mid 1992 this rose to 54 per cent and is expected to rise to 80 per cent of the west German level by 1994 (Müller, 1992). (The convergence of hourly wage rates has been more rapid and parity is expected to be achieved by 1993/4.) Dornbusch and Wolf (1992) give a dramatic illustration of the east German competitiveness problem which has now arisen. They suggest that east German wage costs are on a par with those in the US, and perhaps ten times higher than those of neighbouring eastern European economies, while GDP per employee is at best no better than Mexico or South Korea.

In order to remain competitive with west Germany the east German firms will therefore find it necessary to raise productivity though some observers have already concluded that the east German firms are attempting to achieve the impossible; "To match such a speed of wage convergence, increases in productivity would have to be far beyond the most optimistic predictions"

2

(OECD, 1991a). To the extent that productivity convergence is achieved this will give lessons for other low productivity areas in both eastern and western Europe. One of the main aims of this study was to test how much convergence had already occurred and what were the prospects for future growth.

In addition to making productivity comparisons with west German matched counterparts, comparisons are also made with a low productivity region in western Europe, i.e. Northern Ireland. Other commentators have the noted the potential similarities between the experiences of east Germany and the Italian *Mezzogiorno* given the longstanding nature of industrial policy in southern Italy without any corresponding gains to comparative productivity (Siebert, 1991b). Comparisons with Northern Ireland are of interest for similar sorts of reasons (see below). Manufacturing value added per employee in Northern Ireland has been variously estimated (using statistical sources) as lying between 58 and 72 per cent that of west Germany in 1989 (Census of Production comparisons of net output/gross value added per head in Northern Ireland are compared with the average level for the UK and then linked to the results of studies of the UK-west German productivity gap; the lower estimate for Northern Ireland's comparative productivity derives from Smith, Hitchens and Davies (1982) benchmark for 1968 updated, and the higher estimate from O'Mahoney (1992) for 1987 updated). The causes of the manufacturing productivity shortfall of Northern Ireland relative to west Germany have been investigated in detail (Hitchens, Wagner and Birnie, 1990) and these causes are contrasted with those of east Germany by a process of matched plant comparisons.

Why comparisons of east Germany with Northern Ireland are significant

Since June 1990 east Germany has been experiencing the effects of German Economic and Monetary Union (GEMU), i.e. the relatively weak east German economy has been absorbed by the relatively stronger west German economy and now forms part of a single German currency area. The background to this is that over forty years of the command system and the associated political and economic separation from west Germany has led to a major decline in the comparative living standards of east Germans. Though the extent of this decline remains uncertain. The Council of Economic Advisers together with *Institut der Deutschen Wirtschaft* (Kinsella, 1991) estimate that per capita east German GDP was about 40 per cent that in west Germany in 1988 once price differences are allowed for (PlanEcon estimate that the relationship in 1990 was of a similar order of magnitude; Economist

3

(1991, January 12)).[1] Since west German GDP per capita in 1990 was measured to have been no more than 10 per cent greater than that for the UK at purchasing power standards, it is implied that east German per capita income was about half the UK average or three-fifths the level being attained in Northern Ireland. In other words, the gap is large but not unimaginably so. Northern Ireland along with the Republic of Ireland represent some of the poorest regions within western Europe whilst east Germany (along with Czechoslovakia) is the richest of the former communist bloc with an estimated GDP per capita equivalent to about $8,000 in 1990 as compared to only $5,000 in the former Soviet Union and $4,000 in Poland (PlanEcon; Economist, 1991, January 12).

Since 1989 east German income per head has been subject to a very severe recession such that GDP declined by 42 per cent between 1989 and the start of 1992 (Dornbusch and Wolf, 1992). At the time of writing the latest statistics for the first quarter of 1992 show no improvement in industrial output though some commentators forecast that recovery will begin in 1992 and east Germany will begin to converge rapidly with west Germany (Alexander, 1992).

A long-standing propensity to export people is another common characteristic of the two regions. Northern Ireland has experienced continuous net outmigration since the beginning of the state. In the 1950s the net migration was about 100,000, during the 1960s 70,000, during the 1970s 110,000 and during 1980-85 about 35,000.

Like west Germany, east Germany received an influx of displaced persons at the end of the Second World War. As a result of this the population reached its peak post-war level in 1948 but then began to decline as people began to move to the west. This outmigration continued until the building of the Berlin Wall in 1961 closed off this means of escape from the DDR but total population continued to decline; from 17.068 millions in 1970 to 16.675 millions in 1988. From the middle of 1989 onwards the flow of migrants to the west began to accelerate again and at least half a million east Germans moved to west Germany during 1989 and 1990 (Commission of the European Communities, 1992). One of the effects of GEMU has been to stem what appeared to be a mass exodus to the west but it is likely that the combined effects of continued emigration and a low rate of natural increase will be a decline in the population of east Germany during the 1990s. Outmigration represents a problem for the east German economy to the extent that it represents an outflow of skills. On the other hand, as the east German economy recovers it will be able to benefit by drawing into employment those east Germans who are currently living in the east but are commuting to the west where they gain valuable experience.

The crucial question is whether east Germany post-GEMU will demonstrate more dynamism than the Irish economies have yet to deliver (or indeed, as Barro and Sala-i-Martin (1991) have framed the question, can east Germany deliver a rate of growth much above the relatively low speeds of convergence evidenced by most inter-regional and international examples since the late nineteenth century). East Germany was part of the same economic unit as west Germany until the late 1940s and some regions within east Germany (e.g. Sachsen-Anhalt) would have been characterised by above average levels of economic development by the standards of Germany as a whole whereas other areas (e.g. Mecklenburg-Vorpommern) would historically have been backward. When the two halves of Germany rejoined in 1990 this was equivalent to a sudden shock adjustment for east Germany given that the exchange rate mechanism of adjustment was lost immediately whilst at the same time the home market was opened up to west German firms. A contrast can be drawn with other eastern European economies which have been able to use exchange rate devaluation as a partial response to their problem of inadequate competitiveness on international markets (e.g. Czechoslovakia; Burda (1991)). Whilst, east Germany has in some senses been disadvantaged relative to the rest of eastern Europe given the abruptness of the introduction of the market economy, it is also relatively privileged through its immediate access (to the extent that firms are able to realise this potential) to west German and ultimately European Community consumer and capital markets. Moreover, as Dornbusch and Wolf (1992) argue it is rare for a formerly underdeveloped economy to suddenly be presented with the institutional framework of an advanced economy.

Aims of the study

This study has a number of aims including; to establish the strengths and weaknesses of east German companies, the prospects for their survival, and to recommend industrial policy measures which should be adopted in the light of GEMU. The purpose is to examine how adjustment takes place and the difficulties encountered in order to derive lessons particularly for the eastern European economies which are changing, albeit more slowly, to a market economy and secondly to derive lessons for the other low productivity countries in the EC. More detailed aims of the present work are as follows:

1. To establish a benchmark measure of relative manufacturing productivity in order to examine change amongst a sample of companies in eastern Germany by making comparisons with best practice firms in western Germany and low achievers in the EC represented by Northern Ireland.

5

2. To examine the sources of productivity differences including; machine type, age, technology, utilisation, linking devices, maintenance, breakdowns and manning. Also labour force attitudes including managerial qualifications, labour skills, turnover, absenteeism, work organisation and production networks.

3. Performance and productivity constraints are examined including the supply of raw materials, skilled labour, business services, finance and management, as well as locational difficulties such as transport and logistics. The impact on competitiveness of cost differences especially labour costs are examined in relation to existing productivity performance and change.

4. There is a focus on relative management and labour force qualifications and skills as well as training. Training needs are identified and the constraints on the training process investigated.

5. Particular emphasis is placed on explaining the relative competitive strengths and weaknesses of the east German firms as compared to west German and Northern Ireland counterparts. This includes an investigation of those explanatory factors which have as yet received only a limited coverage in the official statistical sources e.g. the importance of product range, switching of input suppliers from east to west, raised hygiene and product standards, the extent to which the old machine stock (including CNCs) are still usable under new market conditions?

Notes

1. Given the unreliability of national income type statistics in the former communist economies, and problems of conversion between the eastern Net Material Product and western Gross National Product measures and of obtaining suitable standards for comparison of purchasing power, there remains some doubt as to the actual level of output per capita in the DDR on the eve of re-unification. Income per capita in 1988 was estimated as being as high as $12,600 by the United Nations Economic Commission for Europe whereas, using different assumptions about relative purchasing power, Credit Suisse First Boston produced a low estimate of only $4,000 (Commission of the European Communities, 1991). The measurement of east German comparative income per head as being 40 per cent of the level in west Germany would be consistent with an absolute value of $8,000, i.e. roughly half way between these extreme estimates.

2 Methods and descriptions of the sample

This chapter describes the method of inquiry, data sources and objectives of the study.

Method and design of inquiry

The method adopted is one of a matched plant comparison of a wide range of companies relative to their west German and Northern Ireland counterparts. Additional data available from the authors' data banks were used and updated where this was necessary. Companies are matched in terms of product type, process type and post-unification establishment size category. These principal matching criteria allow for an assessment of the efficiency of these east German companies at the time of the visits (April-October 1991).

Questionnaires were developed and tested during April-May, they were especially formulated in order to reflect the special circumstances in east Germany (e.g. higher vertical integration, severe overmanning). An attempt was made to indicate the special problems associated with unification (e.g. the need for investment and consultancy as reflected by the use of producer services) and also to take advantage of any inter-firm comparisons which the east German sample plants had themselves conducted (e.g. consultants reports). The questionnaires considered the change which has already taken place and that which was expected in the near future.

Questions where asked on (a) markets, (b) competitiveness, (c) productivity and sources of productivity (d) determinants of productivity (e.g. strengths and weaknesses of labour, machinery and premises), (e) proposals to improve competitiveness given unification and future wage parity and (f) background data (investment in plant and equipment, finance, ownership, sourcing of raw materials and product improvement).

Choice of sectors

Firms sampled were drawn from five main sectors: engineering; clothing; furniture; food, drink and tobacco (henceforth referred to as food) and miscellaneous trades (which includes electronics, steel, optical, glass and gravel). The purpose was threefold, (a) to represent a cross-section of manufacturing products, skills and technology in east Germany, (b) to represent the strengths and weaknesses of manufacturing in east Germany (see next section) and, (c) to reflect also the cross section of firms sampled (and on the authors' data bases) in west Germany and Northern Ireland.

The structure of east German industry

Table 2.1 examines the structure of manufacturing in east Germany as compared to west Germany. As would be expected, given that the comparison is between a low productivity command economy and a relatively high productivity mixed market economy, significant structural differences are highlighted. The heavier dependence of east Germany on certain sectors reflects in part the tendency of the former member countries of the eastern European Council of Mutual Economic Assistance (CMEA) to specialise on certain economic activities; Ray (1991). There was a larger representation in the DDR of a group of mainly low productivity and low technology level industries such as food etc., textiles and clothing, leather and footwear, and wood and furniture (though the representation of these industries was even stronger in Northern Ireland where they include about half of all those employed in manufacturing). Within this bloc of industry, furniture making has been identified as an activity with relatively good prospects in east Germany (Financial Times, 1989, September 11) given previous links with western retailers (e.g. Ikea in Sweden and MFI in the UK).

8

Table 2.1
Composition of employment,
east Germany and west Germany, 1989
(per cent of total manufacturing)

	EG	WG
Food, drink and tobacco	9.1	6.4
Textiles and clothing	10.2	5.4
Leather and footwear	2.7	0.6
Wood and furniture	4.5	3.5
Paper and paper products	1.6	2.2
Printing and publishing	1.3	2.5
Chemicals	5.9	8.3
Mineral products (e.g. pottery, glass)	9.9	9.2
Metals production	5.6	7.6
Mechanical engineering	15.2	14.0
Vehicle manufacturing	7.2	14.6
Metal goods	8.3	7.0
Electrical engineering	14.2	15.6
Instrument engineering	1.9	1.9
Miscellaneous manufacturing	3.2	1.0

Source: Bode and Krieger-Boden (1990).

In contrast, the chemical industry in east Germany was relatively small when compared to west Germany. IFO (reported in Commerzbank, 1991) considered the east German chemical, petroleum, rubber and plastics industries to have a moderately strong competitive position relative to west Germany but a large technological gap. The engineering and metal industries were relatively heavily represented in both parts of Germany though they were comparatively larger in west Germany (60.7 per cent of total manufacturing employment) compared to east Germany (52.4 per cent). In contrast only 45 per cent of UK manufacturing employees (1988) were employed in the engineering and metals sector and only about one-third of employees in Northern Ireland. Within the general category of engineering, vehicle manufacture was much more strongly represented in the west. East German firms have been judged to have a large technological gap in this activity and a very weak competitive position (Commerzbank, 1991) and in the meantime these plants have been closed down.

The sample

Table 2.2 shows the number of factories sampled by sector in east Germany, west Germany and Northern Ireland.

Table 2.2 Total number of plants visited by sector, east Germany, Northern Ireland and west Germany			
	EG	NI	WG
Engineering	10	12	10
Food	7	5	4
Clothing	3	16	12
Furniture	6	1	1
Miscellaneous*	6	5	7
Total sample	32	39	34

Note: * Electronics, steel, optical, glass, gravel, brushes, packaging and disinfectants.

Profile of east German plants

Firms and sectors (with the exception of clothing and miscellaneous trades) were sampled across all *Länder*, including Berlin, of the former east Germany (Table 2.3). The varying structural characteristics of the economies of the *Länder* made it worthwhile obtaining a sample which was spread across them (Bode and Kreigen-Boden, 1990; *Institut der Deutschen Wirtschaft*, 1991, July 11). The southern *Länder*[1] (Sachsen, Sachsen-Anhalt and Thüringen) were more heavily industrialised than the more agrarian northern *Länder* (Mecklenburg-Vorpommern and Brandenburg) whilst east Berlin had the greatest development of services (Commission of the European Communities, 1992). In Sachsen in 1989 44 per cent of total employment was industrial (defined as including mining) with machinery, light manufacturing and textiles being strongly represented. Electrical and instrument engineering and light manufacturing were strong in Thüringen where 43 per cent of total employment was represented by industry. In Sachsen-Anhalt 39 per cent of total employment was in the industrial sector with chemicals being heavily represented. In Mecklenburg-Vorpommern, Brandenburg and Berlin the share of industry in total employment was less than one-quarter.

Table 2.3
Distribution of plants visited
by sector and location

	M	Br	S	Sa	T	Be	All
Engineering	2	4	0	1	2	1	10
Food	1	2	2	2	0	0	7
Clothing	1	1	0	0	1	0	3
Furniture	1	2	0	1	1	1	6
Miscell.	0	4	1	0	1	0	6
Total	5	13	3	4	5	2	32

Legend: M = Mecklenburg-Vorpommern
Br = Brandenburg
S = Sachsen
Sa = Sachsen-Anhalt
T = Thüringen
Be = Berlin (East)

The three southern *Länder* require restructuring of their manufacturing industries (especially chemicals) (Bode and Kreiger-Boden, 1990) but they are characterised by a good skills base. Thüringen is likely to benefit from proximity to west German industrial centres in Hesse and Bayern. Decline has been forecast for the consumer goods industries based in east Berlin (a switch in consumer spending towards west German products) and service employment will fall as overmanning is removed. Farming in Mecklenburg

11

and Brandenburg will have the problem of trying to adapt to the conditions of general oversupply in the EC.

Table 2.4
Size distribution of sample plants before and after unification

	Before unification	After unification
under 50	2	6
50 - under 100	4	2
100 - under 500	6	11
500 - under 1000	7	3
1000 - under 3000	3	7
3000 - under 5000	6	1
5000 and more	4	2
Total sample	32	32

Plants were sampled across the wide size range which was present both before and after unification (Table 2.4). When these are compared on a matched basis in Table 2.5 a similar spread is shown for each area. It is important to note the study matched *plants* and not firms. In the DDR companies were typically the giant *Kombinate* (in 1989 there were 120 of these with an average employment size of 25,000; Bryson and Melzer, 1991). These have subsequently been broken up by the *Treuhand* and it is these much reduced plant sizes that have been identified in the comparison considered here.

Table 2.6 shows the average size of plants by sector before and after unification and compares these averages with west Germany and Northern Ireland (NI).

Table 2.5
Size distribution of plants
compared between samples
(per cent of total sample)

Employees	EG	WG	NI
under 50	20	13	14
50 - under 100	7	29	8
100 - under 500	37	36	60
500 - under 1000	10	6	9
1000 - under 3000	23	13	6
3000 - under 5000	3	3	3
5000 and more	0	0	0
Total sample	100	100	100

Table 2.6
Average size of plant by sector
(number of employees)

	EG			WG 1988	NI 1988
	Before unification	After unification	Predicted end 1992		
Engineering	1,987	959	675	693	471
Food	543	228	198	440	690
Clothing	572	434	357	204	311
Furniture	737	365	288	266	60

The number of east German processes or products matched was 75 per cent, whilst a sectoral match was obtained in 80 per cent of cases. Hence, nearly all the western data base could be contrasted with the east German companies sampled. The match by size is more difficult to interpret because of restructuring of east German industry. For example, as the above table shows the predicted rate of employment decline at the time of the interview (e.g. by two-thirds in engineering) suggests that no precise figure can be given on the proportion of firms which are identical to their western counterparts, nevertheless their predicted average sizes are broadly comparable to those in west Germany and Northern Ireland. Where necessary on critical variables subsamples are compared and the commentary following will refer to relevant firm and plant matches where these are sensitive to the matching criteria.

Ownership

<table>
<tr><td colspan="4">Table 2.7
East German sample plants privatised*
with location of new ownership</td></tr>
<tr><td></td><td>Total</td><td colspan="2">Privatised</td></tr>
<tr><td></td><td></td><td>EG</td><td>WG</td></tr>
<tr><td>Engineering</td><td>10</td><td>1</td><td>2</td></tr>
<tr><td>Food</td><td>7</td><td>1</td><td>2</td></tr>
<tr><td>Clothing</td><td>3</td><td>0</td><td>1</td></tr>
<tr><td>Furniture</td><td>6</td><td>2</td><td>2</td></tr>
<tr><td>Miscellaneous</td><td>6</td><td>0</td><td>2</td></tr>
<tr><td>Total sample</td><td>32</td><td>4</td><td>9</td></tr>
</table>

Note: * As of January 1992 this includes two companies privatised since our visit.

Table 2.7 shows the ownership of plants sampled. Forty per cent of companies sampled have been privatised of which 69 per cent were taken over by west German companies. This compares with the overall rate of privatisation by the *Treuhand* of 48.6 per cent by August 1991. At the time of writing there are still a large number of companies under the control of the *Treuhand* representing more than one million employees in July 1992 though this was two-thirds fewer than in January 1991 (Söstra, 1992).

In summary the aim of the work has been to draw a representative sample of east German manufacturing industry stratified by sector, size, location and ownership before a consideration is given to the matched counterparts in west Germany and Northern Ireland.

Notes

1.   The regional variations in extent of industrialisation in east Germany are considered at the level of the *Länder* even though the communist authorities abolished this layer of administration in 1952. The five *Länder* were recreated in 1990 along with a unified administration for the city of Berlin.

3 Comparative company performance

Productivity: Measures of levels

Three methods were used to assess the comparative productivity level attained in the east German sample plants.

First, the firms visited were asked to supply data on the physical output (i.e. volume, weight or number of units) of the major products of the plant. The implied physical productivity could be compared with the results derived from the authors' own data bank relating to the earlier visits to companies in west Germany. In some cases the firms were able to quote the results of consultants' studies which had compared their productivity with that achieved by west German firms. Alternatively, some west German firms provided assessments of east German productivity.

Second, the comparative physical productivity results were used to infer differences in levels of value added per employee. We define potential value added per employee as that which can be achieved given physical productivity differences estimated and actual product price differences recorded by firms, assuming east German firms are working at the same capacity utilisation of their west German counterparts. Industrial Census data were used to compare average manufacturers' prices for the products of the sample sectors (these were checked against, and confirmed by, sample plant responses). In general east German unit prices were estimated to be substantially lower than those ruling in west Germany. Thus the potential comparative value added per head of east German manufacturing (i.e. the relative performance which could theoretically be achieved under very favourable assumptions about equivalent use of capacity) is implied to be lower than the comparative level of physical productivity to the extent that average prices are lower. The lower output price recorded for east Germany reflects several factors; the severe slump in orders for the east German firms is likely to have led to price cutting relative to western producers making identical products, and within each broad census category it is likely that the east German firms produce generally lower quality and lower price goods. These results will tend to underestimate the east German comparative value added per head to the extent that the Census price differences arise from price cutting.

Thirdly, the actual productivity record of the firms was measured, i.e. sales per employee were compared. This performance index was strongly influenced by fluctuations in activity at the plant over the period, e.g. a sudden loss of markets has in many cases severely depressed the actual value added per head.

Table 3.1
Comparative east German productivity by sample sector, mid 1991 (as % of level of matched west German counterparts, EG/WG, WG=100)

	Physical Producti- vity	Potential value added per head	Actual value per head
Engineering	64	51	37
Food	60	56	40
Clothing	50	29	27
Furniture	63	44	56[a]
Miscellaneous*	58	51	33
Total sample	59	46	33

Notes: * In this table and, unless otherwise stated, in the following tables sectoral results are unweighted averages of the results for individual firms.
[a] Orders from the Soviet Union (guaranteed by the German government under the Hermes programme) pushed the 1990-91 performance of some furniture firms above its likely long run level.

Table 3.1 shows the result. The actual productivity levels being achieved in mid 1991 lay between one-quarter and two-fifths of those in the west German counterparts (because of a short-lived boom in orders the furniture firms were able to do unusually well and achieve levels of output per head more than half as high as those in the west). The estimate of comparative productivity in the clothing firms accords with an alternative estimate of 30 per cent and in some exceptional cases 50 per cent (*Handelsblatt*, 1991, May 1). IFO (1991) reckon that east German manufacturing productivity was about one-third of the west German level in the fourth quarter of 1990.

Productivity growth

Productivity change in the year since German monetary and economic union (i.e. June 1990) could be calculated by asking the firms about employment and output change. When the index of productivity change was applied to the comparative productivity results for 1991 it was possible to imply the east German comparative performance in mid 1990.

One of the most notable results to be drawn from Table 3.2 is that the underlying productivity performance (i.e. excluding the impact of the sudden decline in orders) of the east German sample firms has on average improved by almost 50 per cent since June 1990. This indication of a strong improvement in underlying productivity performance (i.e. the growth of output per head on production lines which continued in use throughout 1990-91) is not inconsistent with the results of other sources. For example, output per hour has been estimated to have grown 76 per cent during January-December 1991 (DIW, 1992). However, the achieved value added per employee of east German firms has probably gained much less ground relative to west German counterparts once the recession in demand is allowed for and hence the impact of closure of production lines or whole plants. The official statistical sources imply that the actual productivity of east German manufacturing as a whole declined slightly (by 4 per cent) during June 1990-June 1991 given that the decline in output (42 per cent) was marginally greater than the reduction in employment (40 per cent); DIW (1991a, 1991b).

Table 3.2
Productivity change in east German sample,
1990-91
(per cent change)

	Mid-1990/ mid-1991		Comparative potential* value added per head	
	Output	Employ-ment	Mid 1990	Mid 1991
Food	+4	-57	23	56
Engineering	-59	-66	41	51
Clothing	-13	-39	20	29
Furniture	-36	-47	36	44
Miscellaneous	-46	-62	36	51
Total sample	-32	-53	31	46

Note: * In early 1990 the actual performance of the east German firms would have been closer to the potential, i.e. the firms were still operating at a level near to full capacity.

In every sector the sample plants experienced substantial losses of employment during June 1990-mid 1991. Except for clothing and furniture the sectoral employments in mid 1990 were generally less than half what they had been a year before. According to the official statistics total employment in east German manufacturing declined from 3.24 million in mid 1990 (the average of the second and third quarters) to just under 2 million by mid 1991, i.e. a decline of 40 per cent.

The following table compares the sample sectoral output changes with those implied by the aggregate official data (i.e. indices of industrial production). The table shows that in every sector except food the sample results are very close to those indicated by the official statistics, e.g. engineering experiences a massive fall in production whereas in clothing the decline is more modest. On average the sample firms experienced an output decline of almost one-third which appears somewhat better than the performance of east German manufacturing as a whole as implied by the index of production (an output decline of 42-44 per cent). There are several reasons for this discrepancy.

Table 3.3
Output change in east Germany, mid 1990-mid 1991,
sample results compared with official statistics
(per cent change)

	Sample	Index of production[*]
Food	+4	-7
Engineering	-59	-57[a]
Clothing	-13	-20[b]
Furniture	-36	-38
Miscellaneous	-32	-44[c]
Total	-32	-44[d] -42[e]

Notes: [*] Given changes in the definition of the east German output series these indices are based on July 1990 and show output decline to June 1991.
[a] A weighted average of mechanical, electrical and instrument engineering.
[b] Clothing combined with textiles.
[c] A weighted average of mineral products, iron and steel, chemicals and paper and printing industries.
[d] A weighted average of all the individual sectors included in this table.
[e] Definition of total manufacturing used by the statistical authorities (this includes some sectors not considered here).

First, the sample firms in food recorded a growth in output while the official statistics suggest that the industry as a whole was in decline (two of those sampled had responded rapidly to unification by introducing modern equipment). Second, the weights of the different sectors within the sample differ from the weights of those industries within total manufacturing (e.g. clothing firms represented a larger proportion of the sample than the output share of clothing in manufacturing would have warranted). Given these structural differences, less attention should be paid to the aggregate sample output change than to the results for the individual industries.

A third reason why the sample might have been expected to return a better output performance than manufacturing as a whole is that it represents a group of companies which have survived throughout this period. The output of east German manufacturing has declined not only because of change within the body of survivors but because the number of firms within that group has shrunk.

Productivity: Variability in the levels achieved

Table 3.4 illustrates the range of comparative productivity performances within the sample of east German companies. At more than half the plants visited estimated physical productivity is at a level of 60 per cent or more that of the west German counterparts. However, only about one-third could potentially achieve more than 60 per cent of west German value added per employee given the value of their products and only about one-fifth were actually achieving that level of productivity.

At the other end of the scale whilst just one-fifth had physical productivity estimated at below 50 per cent that of west Germany, when account is taken of product values this proportion rises to nearly one-half of the sample. Those companies which could be identified as likely long term survivors (see below) had above average physical, potential and actual productivity performance.

It is important to stress that these observations on productivity levels and change relate only to those companies which have survived German monetary and economic union up to the time of the plant visits. For example, it could be assumed that the proportion of east German plants with physical productivities less than half those of their west German counterparts would have been even higher in November 1989 or June 1990 than in June 1991. Many of the low productivity plants would already have closed during June 1990- June 1991. Thus the distribution of plants (by comparative performance) observed in June 1991 is truncated in contrast with the original DDR distribution. A possibly long tail of low efficiency plants has already been removed from the distribution (Salter, 1966). One would expect to observe this effect on manufacturing performance in a western economy in a recession; the so-called "productivity miracle" of the 1980s in UK manufacturing is sometimes attributed in part to this "batting average" effect: plants with below average productivity shut down which raises the average productivity of those which remain (Muellbauer, 1986). However, in the unusual circumstances of east Germany these effects have been felt with special ferocity.

22

Table 3.4
Distribution of east German plants according to
comparative productivity achieved
(per cent of sample plants)

	Comparative productivity		
	> 60% of WG	50-60% of WG	< 50% of WG
Physical productivity	56	22	22
Potential value added per head	32	31	47
Actual value added per head	19	9	72

Comparison of productivity levels: East Germany compared to Northern Ireland

Previous research by the authors has established Northern Ireland as a region with one of the lowest levels of manufacturing productivity throughout the western market economies (Hitchens, Wagner and Birnie, 1990). During the last 70 years levels of output per head have been 20-30 per cent lower than those attained by manufacturing in the rest of the UK. By implication, Northern Ireland has been characterised by a very substantial lag in productivity relative to examples of best practice in western Europe, e.g. west Germany. It is of interest to compare east Germany, a former planned economy in transition to the market economy, with Northern Ireland, a market economy which has consistently had a poor productivity performance.

Table 3.5 compares statistical measures of Northern Ireland's comparative value added per employee with those results obtained from the sample study of east German plants.

Table 3.5
Manufacturing productivity (value added per head), east Germany and Northern Ireland

NI/WG (WG=100)	EG/WG (WG=100)		EG/NI[c] (NI=100)	
1989	1990	1991	1990	1991
58-72[a]		33[b]		(46-57)[b]
	(31)[d]	(46)[d]	(43-53)[d]	(63-79)[d]

Notes: [a] Census of Production measures of NI productivity compared to the UK average are linked to results of international comparisons. Lower figure derives from Smith, Hitchens and Davies (1982, updated) and higher figure from O'Mahoney (1992).
[b] Comparisons relating to actual value added at the sample EG plants given the current depression of demand.
[c] Approximate results since it was assumed that the NI/WG comparative productivity level remained constant during 1989-91.
[d] Comparisons relating to potential value added per head if the sample EG plants were operating at normal utilisation.

These results suggest that not only have the east German firms made up ground relative to their west German counterparts but there has been marked progress in narrowing the gap relative to Northern Ireland manufacturing. In the year between mid-1990 and mid-1991 it is implied that between one-third and 55 per cent of the productivity differential between the two areas was removed. The speed of such change stands in marked contrast to Northern Ireland's historical performance which has been one of only gradual convergence with productivity levels in the rest of the UK let alone with those levels in continental western Europe.

Productivity change in the second half of 1991 at sample plants

Eighty-four per cent of sample plants were recontacted at the end of 1991 to establish their performance six months on. These further results will be referred to later. With respect to productivity change an overall gain of 6.4 per cent was indicated. No change was shown in the food sector, the better performance was divided between the engineering and miscellaneous trades.

Expected improvements in productivity performance

Individual firms were asked how physical productivity levels could be raised towards west German standards. The following table shows where these gains were expected to come from.

Table 3.6
Sources of expected productivity gains by the east German plants

	Current compara- tive physical produc- tivity (WG=100)	Sources of expected gains (per cent point gains)		Expected compara- tive physical produc- tivity (WG=100)
		Machinery[a]	Training[b]	
Food	60	24	12	96
Engineering	64	13	6	82
Clothing	50	9	9	68
Furniture	63	18	14	95
Miscellan- eous	58	10	8	76
Total sample	59	16	9	84

Notes: [a] New machinery, technology, machine add-ons and application of data processing.
[b] Training and work organisation.

This table shows that on average the east German firms anticipate that they can raise their physical productivity from 59 per cent to 84 per cent of the level in west Germany. In food and furniture the east German plant managers were able to envisage their plants achieving levels of physical productivity roughly the same as those at their west German counterparts. However, in engineering, clothing and miscellaneous a very substantial productivity gap would persist even if the anticipated productivity

25

improvements were realised. This suggests that the managers in those sectors did not know how productivity could be fully raised to west German levels. In every sector except clothing, investment in physical capital and technology was anticipated to yield larger productivity gains than those which would be realised from training and reorganisation of work. Hence the final closing of the gap may require much greater improvements in human capital than can be foreseen at present by management in the east and is more pronounced in engineering, clothing and miscellaneous trades. Arguably capital deficiencies are much more obvious to the eastern managers. This is independent of further improvements required to close the value added gap and improve product quality.

This lower priority given to the human side of the business is further confirmed in an answer to the question what is the cause of the poor productivity? The main reason given in 59 per cent of cases was old machinery, technology and consequent breakdowns. In 27 per cent of cases labour and management related factors including training, organisation, overmanning and attitudes and, in a further 14 per cent of cases, a poor product.

Contrast with the explanatory factors in Northern Ireland

In the sample survey of firms in Northern Ireland labour related factors were cited in 42 per cent of cases as the main explanation for the productivity gap relative to west Germany. This contrasts with only 27 per cent of east German firms citing labour and management related factors. The importance of this group of factors for the Northern Ireland firms testifies to problems of overmanning and restrictions on labour flexibility which were more marked than those found in the east German firms at the time of the visits (much of the overmanning in the east German firms had already been removed during 1990-91 or management had plans to remove it in the near future).

A further difference between the east German and Northern Ireland firms was that in the Northern Ireland sample machinery related factors were a relatively minor explanation of the productivity gap relative to west Germany (cited by 28 per cent of firms) whereas in the east German sample capital related explanations were cited in 59 per cent of cases. This contrast is indicative of the relatively old age and technological backwardness of the east German capital stock (see below). It was notable that when the Northern Ireland firms were asked what was the main cause of their growth over a five year period most respondents cited either management (19 per cent) or labour related (e.g. manning rates, work organisation and training) factors

26

(37 per cent). Only a minority of Northern Ireland firms stressed machinery as a cause of productivity growth (37 per cent) whereas for most of the east German firms growth related to capital was anticipated to be the main source of future productivity gains. And when a sub-sample of the Northern Ireland firms (numbering 24) were revisited in 1991 and asked to forecast what would be the main sources of future productivity improvement, training and methods were cited in 52 per cent of cases but machinery in only 35 per cent (the remaining factors were product related, e.g. design or the level of demand). The fact that the managers in east Germany placed much more emphasis on growth coming from new machinery underlines the weakness of the machine stock in east Germany relative to Northern Ireland.

Capacity utilisation

The levels of capacity utilisation at the time of the company visits is shown in Table 3.7 (these are after the slimming down of operations and excluding short-time[1] working).

The table shows that capacity utilisation is well below that of west German companies in all sectors. It is highest in food and lowest in engineering. The Northern Ireland comparisons indicate that in two especially weak sectors, engineering and miscellaneous trades, capacity utilisation was also low (though not to the same extent as the east German counterparts). Expected survivors in all sectors had on average higher capacity utilisation with the greatest difference being shown by the survivors in engineering and furniture production.

Table 3.7 Capacity utilisation by sector (per cent)		
	EG	WG	NI
Food	69	100	93
Engineering	34	89	69
Clothing	50	95	85
Furniture	47	85[*]	63[*]
Miscellaneous	56	85[*]	63[*]

Note: [*] Furniture and miscellaneous trades combined.

The extent of shiftworking has also fallen since unification. The following table shows that on average the number of shifts worked has halved over the period.

Table 3.8 Shiftworking at sample east German plants (number of shifts)		
	Mid 1990	Mid 1991
Food	2.5	1.4
Engineering	2.4	1.2
Clothing	1.0	1.0
Furniture	2.7	2.0
Miscellaneous	3.2	1.2

Product range, materials, product quality

Firms were asked how their product range had been altered since unification. Only one-third narrowed their ranges, one-third left them unchanged, one-quarter engaged in further diversification and the rest changed their products. Seventy-four per cent of firms also reduced their batch sizes. Prior to unification most east German firms were producing very long runs of identical products.

All companies were characterised by a high degree of vertical integration prior to unification (as part of the *Kombinate* formed after 1972; Bryson and Melzer, 1991; Collier and Siebert, 1991) and had since reduced the degree of self-sufficiency by increasing use of outside suppliers. Where firms had discontinued vertically integrated activities (e.g. manufacture of castings, assembly of electronics and manufacture of own machinery) and now relied on specialist suppliers gains were reported in terms of the price and quality of inputs.

The type of material inputs also changed. Two-thirds of companies reported using better quality raw materials. Clothing was being made from lighter and better materials and in furniture superior chipboard was now being used. Previously where such inputs were of a poor quality the planning system required that they should still be incorporated in the manufacturing process. Under market conditions the firms now had the scope to reject materials of unacceptable quality. In general components (e.g. hinges and springs) were more up to date.

At all the firms visited many raw materials were bought from western suppliers in order to obtain inputs of better specification, quality and more reliable delivery. East German companies were less likely to be used as suppliers (largely because of uncertainty surrounding their future survival).

Difficulties in forecasting future demand made it difficult for sample companies to obtain bulk discounts from suppliers and moreover they claimed informational disadvantages with regard to knowing the price of raw materials and components. Nevertheless material costs and costs of capital goods have fallen for most of the east German firms. These price changes were judged by; (a) the input price relative to the product selling price and relative to the pre-unification price of other inputs, (b) the difference between the pre-unification-unification *Ost Mark*-DM exchange rate and the one-for-one parity imposed by German monetary union. In fact one third of sample firms were able to quote the extent of material cost savings. Half of them quoted items which were now 75 per cent cheaper whilst all claimed savings of more than 20 per cent.

Seventy-eight per cent of firms sampled improved the quality of their products post-unification[2], with rather more of those predicted to survive doing so. These improvements included better electronic controls, use of DIN standards, use of better raw materials (e.g. chipboard, steel), better machining, more rigorous quality control systems etc. In another sample study (*Institut der Deutschen Wirtschaft*, 1991) 40 per cent of 200 companies interviewed had acquired quality certificates for their goods (this is probably the easiest way to achieve higher quality standards: the requirements are fixed and given).

Packaging was investigated in the case of the food companies visited and the majority of these (70 per cent) improved their packaging, with a better use of materials, the integration of design, offering a variety of sizes and in one case adapting to west German standards on environmental protection.

Structure of employment change at plants

Table 3.9 shows the structure of employment at the time of the plant visits.

Table 3.9				
Shop-floor employment composition of plants sampled, east Germany (per cent of total plant employment)				
		Shop-floor		
	Total	of which		
		Meister/ foremen	Main-tenance	Appren-tices
Engineering	64	6	-	23
Food, drink and tobacco	65	3	-	11
Clothing	78	6	-	14
Furniture	56	5	-	5
Miscellaneous	77	7	-	13
Total sample	67	5	7	13

Note: These sectoral average data represent unweighted averages of all the firms for which the data was available.

In addition to changes in the total numbers employed since unification the components of that change were considered, namely in the direct (or shop-floor) workers and those working in maintenance or as apprentices or *Meister* (foremen).

Turning now to changes in the different categories of employment, Table 3.10 shows the reductions which have occurred since unification.

It has already been seen that overall employment has roughly halved since unification. Table 3.10 shows that the employment of direct workers (i.e. shop-floor, apprentices and *Meister*) has generally declined by a slightly smaller amount. The decline among the direct workers includes those who formerly worked in the social services attached to the factories, vocational schools, political appointees, management and maintenance (the latter are

30

shown in the table; the decline in the numbers of maintenance workers was especially severe which is unsurprising given one estimate that in the late 1980s 17 per cent of the labour force of industry in DDR was engaged in maintenance work (Bryson and Melzer, 1991)).

Whilst for the sample as a whole the employment of *Meister* held up better than overall employment this was not true of engineering, clothing and furniture (in practice the *Meister* sometimes continued in employment but had been downgraded because of a lack of skill (but see below)). The proportion of apprentices in total employment remains similar to that at unification, the *Treuhand* adopted a policy to maintain apprentice training at those firms over which they had authority.

Table 3.10
Reduction in shop-floor employment
(employment level at visit as per cent at unification)

	Total	*Meister*	Apprentices	Maintenance
Engineering	64	38	47	42
Food	57	90	95	50
Clothing	81	50	-	40
Furniture	49	39	52	45
Miscellaneous	43	73	58	9
Total sample	55	54	55	30

Note: Sectoral averages are weighted.

A continued reduction in employment is planned to 1992/3 with again greater emphasis reported by managers on the need to decrease employment amongst the indirects. Significantly the small firms included in the sample tended to forecast an increase in their employment. The forecast is shown in Table 3.11 alongside December 1991 levels.

Table 3.11
Employment change in sample plants
(level in mid 1990=100)

	Mid 1991	End 1991	End 1992*
Food	43	41	37
Engineering	34	29	24
Clothing	61	59	50
Furniture	53	52	42
Miscellaneous	38	32	28
Total sample	47	43	36

Note: * As forecast by 85% of the sample plants in June 1991.

The data in the table indicate that the rate of actual employment decline as shown for the end of 1991 is broadly at the same rate as that predicted in mid 1991 for the end of 1992.

Employment comparisons with west Germany and Northern Ireland

Table 3.12 shows the composition of employment at Northern Ireland and west German matched plants. It shows that on average the proportion of direct workers in both areas was higher than in east Germany (this was despite the fact that the Northern Ireland and West German firms had larger commercial labour forces, e.g. sales and marketing). Comparison with east Germany also suggests that the west German firms employed fewer *Meister* whereas the NI plants had a larger number of supervisors/foremen.

Table 3.12 (a)
Sample comparisons of employment
composition by sector
(% of total employment)

	Shop-floor		R & D	
	WG	NI	WG	NI
Engineering	74	71	-	-
Food	71	65	-	-
Clothing	81	78	-	-
Furniture	67	70	-	-
Total sample	73	71	5.0	1.5

Table 3.12 (b)
Sample comparisons of employment
composition by sector
(% of shop-floor employment)

	Meister/ foremen*		Apprentices		Maintenance	
	WG	NI	WG	NI	WG	NI
Engineering	6	10	9	1	-	-
Food	6	6	3	-	-	-
Clothing	2	5	15	-	-	-
Furniture	3	4	5	-	-	-
Total sample	4	6	7	1	4	10

Notes: Sectoral figures are unweighted averages.
* German Meister with their lengthy formal training are being compared with foremen/supervisors in NI which are usually only time served.

Market changes

Table 3.13 shows that the east German sample firms have lost markets in eastern Europe. For east German manufacturing as a whole exports to eastern countries fell by 60 per cent between 1989 and 1991. There were two major reasons for collapse of sales to the other eastern European economies. First, the depression of these economies reduced demand. Second, the eastern European countries were now required to deal with east Germany in DM terms and in hard currency.

The sales to the former USSR since unification have been dependent on west German government guarantees and credit arrangements and there is a continued vulnerability to political disruption of these markets (e.g. the moves to independence by some of the Soviet Republics led to orders for the east German sample firms being postponed). The sample firms in engineering, furniture and clothing experienced the worst reductions in eastern European demand.

The proportion of sales going to the "home", i.e. former DDR, market remained stable at 58 per cent. Sales going to the west and particularly west Germany had increased; the re-orientation to the western markets was greatest in engineering, food and clothing. In another sample study about 20 per cent of 200 companies were reported to have exported to the EC (excluding west Germany); *Institut der Deutschen Wirtschaft* (1991, November 7).

The official statistics suggest that before unification (1988) exports represented 24 per cent of manufacturing sales (more than half of exports went to eastern bloc economies). The external sales of machinery were higher (37 per cent) and more than four-fifths of these exports were directed to the command economies.

Table 3.13
Market breakdown of sales pre- and post
unification
(per cent of total sales)

	EG	East Europe & USSR*	WG	Other western markets
Engineering				
post unification	66	17	16	2
pre-unification	41	56	4**	
Food				
post unification	70	5	21	4
pre-unification	94	2	3**	
Clothing				
post unification	40	0	60	0
pre-unification	47	20	33**	
Furniture				
post unification	52	16	2	31
pre-unification	42	31	28**	
Miscellaneous				
post unification	50	19	21	11
pre-unification	59	19	23**	
Total sample				
post unification	58	13	25	4
pre-unification	58	27	15**	

Notes: * In the second half of 1990 exports to the then Soviet Union increased very substantially because the German government supported these exports through subsidising the number of DM which each Rouble could buy. The government also, temporarily, covered the losses of the east German exporters which now had costs on the basis of one *Ost Mark* to one DM. 1,600 companies applied for support of a total 6 billion DM (DIW, 1991a).

** Includes other western markets.

Summary

This chapter has considered three measures of the comparative productivity of firms in east Germany as well as productivity change over time and a number of direct determinants of the productivity level (especially the effect of market changes on capacity utilisation). Physical productivity assuming normal levels of plant utilisation was found to be three-fifths that of west Germany and comparable to the levels attained by sample firms in Northern Ireland. The managers of the east German plants expected this could be raised to 84 per cent that of west Germany with investment in machinery and labour. A significant difficulty for the east German companies is the comparatively poor quality of products which reduces value added per head relative to west Germany. The loss of eastern European and former USSR markets has also depressed levels of capacity utilisation and the actual level of productivity achieved.

Notes

1.   In the case of east Germany short-time working refers to companies being legally obliged to retain on the payroll workers whose jobs would otherwise become redundant.

2.   Under the DDR regime there had been repeated and largely unsuccessful attempts to raise the quality of east German products. The Eleventh Party Conference decreed that 60 per cent of final consumption goods should reach western standards by 1990 (Bryson and Melzer, 1991). There was also a drive to "all-encompassing intensification", i.e. innovation. Despite these efforts the comparative quality of east German products continued to drop which was indicated by the decline of the relative unit price of east German exports in western market (i.e. the goods were falling into lower market positions; The Economist, 1988, July 30). At unification Akerlof, Rose, Yellen and Hessenius (1991) estimated that almost no east German products would be competitive on quality and price on western markets in the absence of prices subsidies.

4 Prospects for the future

This chapter examines the likely competitiveness of east German sample plants within a market economy and gives special consideration of their prospects for survival.

Firm advantages and disadvantages

Whilst there was little variation between the sectors in the number of competitive advantages claimed more disadvantages were claimed by engineering companies than by firms in the other four sectors sampled.

The types of competitive advantage could be divided into two broad groups. The first (claimed in 27 per cent of cases) was the presence of a good skill base (particularly in the cases of the engineering and miscellaneous trades). The second most important advantage (23 per cent) was knowledge of, and connections with, the CMEA markets (especially in the furniture, engineering and miscellaneous trades). Low wages were cited in 10 per cent of cases (though largely offset by low productivity). In a small number of cases (10 per cent) the stock of machinery was said to be an advantage (this applied to companies which even before unification had some west German machinery and trading arrangements with western markets). In 13 per cent of cases experience of western contractors was cited. Locational advantages were claimed in 13 per cent and other factors were cited by 8 per cent of the firms.

The disadvantages could also be divided into two large groups. The most important related to the product and its market and involved 35 per cent of disadvantages (e.g. loss of markets in eastern Europe, poor quality and image, uncompetitiveness on price, and lack of marketing expertise). The second main group concerned production facilities (cited in 26 per cent of cases) and included old machinery and technology, lack of automation, poor buildings and high production costs. Engineering, clothing and miscellaneous trades emphasised the demand side factors which reflected their loss of eastern markets and difficulty in penetrating the west with required design and product standards. (Demand side growth constraints have been noted by the DIW (1991a) amongst steel, electrical, shipbuilding, chemicals, textiles, clothing, shoes and toys.) Whilst supply side factors were emphasised by engineering and food companies (supply side factors such as materials, work organisation, marketing and packaging were also stressed in another sample study of 200 east German firms; *Institut der Deutschen Wirtschaft* (1991)).

An analysis of business plans indicates that the principal priority concerned rectifying supply side problems especially regarding new investment. Table 4.1 shows that the priority in current and recent investment has been given to new equipment.

Table 4.1
Investment priorities
(per cent of total cases)

New machinery, technology etc.	63
Building and premises	27
Environmental compliance	10

In terms of the business plans themselves half gave greatest priority to investment in physical capital. Just over a quarter were concerned to improve product market performance (e.g. quality, after sales service). A similar proportion were concerned with improving productivity.

Product competitiveness and the survival of firms

It was of interest to divide firms with very poor prospects of survival (as judged both by their own management and by comparison with western counterparts) from others sampled. We have made a modest and conservative attempt to distinguish firms which looked very likely to survive from the rest. Those judged likely to survive had more competitive products and were

38

more likely to have ties with west German manufacturers. Table 4.2 shows
the results of this analysis.

Table 4.2 Number of plants likely to survive			
	Survivors (%)*	Closures	Unknown
Engineering	4 (40)	3	3
Food	4 (57)	2	1
Clothing	2 (67)	1	0
Furniture	3 (50)	2	1
Miscellaneous	4 (67)	1	1
Total sample	17 (53)	9	6

Note: * Survival rate within each sector.

(a) Engineering

The four plants which were recognised as potential survivors include one
which had initially a strong product positioning before unification. Two
others had been bought by leading west German counterparts which were
anxious to increase their market share in the east (these purchases were
facilitated by the fact of previous close product connections and market
positions). The fourth engineering survivor is a small company which would
be likely to survive on a local market.

(b) Clothing

Two of the three clothing companies visited are expected to survive entirely
because of the intervention by a leading west German supplier of that type
of garment. This has led to the use of modern materials, newer designs,
better training, improved sewing and more punctual delivery. In one of these
companies 95 per cent of machines had been replaced so as to facilitate high
quality and efficient production.

(c) Food

Four of the seven food factories are likely to survive. Two of these potential survivors are plants which have been taken over by west German companies (in one case because a market is guaranteed by local taste and in the other because transport costs are too high for a producer in west Germany selling into the east German market). In a further case a product change together with new and appropriate equipment is likely to ensure survival. In the final case a strong local market makes survival probable.

(d) Furniture

Three furniture companies are expected to survive and all of these are cooperating with major west German producers. One had strong exports to the west prior to unification, one was a high quality producer by east German standards, another had a similarly high quality range to which its other products could be raised (though these products would be considered medium to low standard on the west German market) and the third was a local producer (a fourth may survive in some very reduced form and is presently employing 349 people).

(e) Miscellaneous

Four of the six miscellaneous companies are expected to survive. Two had strong western market positions prior to unification and have partnerships with major western companies. The other two have strong local markets. Additionally, in two of the four cases firms visited were the single most important regional employers and as such are likely to enjoy considerable subsidy assistance from the state.

(f) Likely failures

From the foregoing it can be seen that the market has already begun to sift out those firms which are likely to succeed. These are the ones which have come under west German ownership or are now in partnership with western producers and where this has happened there has nearly always been considerable investment in plant and machinery, training and product development. It is unlikely that an eastern ownership will develop in many cases other than in the small firm sector.

At the same time, not all plants with western partners will necessarily survive, there were examples in engineering and clothing which appear to have been weakened by relatively poor western management. Those plants that are likely to fail had a range of problems. For example, poor quality, and an inability to reach market requirements with regard to marketing, advertising, design, user-friendliness and packaging. Some product lines in a minority of cases will fail because they are redundant (e.g. hand tailoring) or because of overcapacity among the western economies (examples include sewing machines and micro-chips). In some cases production techniques were several generations out of date. Further consideration is given to these matters below.

Predicted performance of survivors

While forecasts made by managers should be treated with extreme caution, potential survivors were asked to forecast their growth of output and employment to the end of 1992. These indicated that the value added per employee of those firms likely to survive in the east German sample will reach four-fifths of the current west German level by the end of 1992 (this was equivalent to more than doubling the present level of productivity at those east German factories). It was anticipated that the level of employment would drop to 53 per cent of the level in mid 1990 while productivity would increase by 111 per cent.

Problems associated with failing and surviving firms

All the sample firms foresaw problems in the future, all suffered financial problems especially for investment and working capital and all were required to modify their products for the western market. To varying extents all required modernisation of equipment and technology, shop-floor training and installation of management expertise. Those that are predicted to fail either had more, or more intense, difficulties than those in the group of probable survivors. The emphasis of their problems differed too.

In fact, on average five separate major technical, product or market difficulties were identified amongst the failing group as against three in the surviving group. In general fewer problems associated with marketing were identified amongst the surviving group and fewer technical problems too. Half of those companies in the group of survivors were already selling to the west prior to unification as compared to only 5 per cent amongst the likely failures.

The main problems amongst the likely failures (noted in more than half of cases) related to the product and especially quality, design, durability, reject rates, working to required standards and lack of use of west German

41

electronics.

In the group of firms judged as likely to fail there were also three times as many problems associated with their market, e.g. overcapacity in the world market, the low probability of recapturing old markets or finding replacements, a lack of price competitiveness and dearth of new products or new ideas. When problems identified with products are added to these market difficulties they sum to three-quarters of the reasons given as to why these companies are likely to collapse.

In contrast product design and marketing problems were identified as constraints at one-eighth of a similar sample of west German firms whilst nearly half of the Northern Ireland firms sampled had difficulties with their markets and especially their products which constrained growth and competitiveness. This is indicative of the fact that the Northern Ireland firms like their east German counterparts often suffered from growth constraints arising from the poor quality of their products.

The extent of adjustment already made to post unification market requirements

(a) Product quality

Quality has improved at three-quarters of the plants sampled but in half of these cases they have still to attain west German standards and thereby were not achieving the value added of their western counterparts. The quality improvements achieved to date included greater durability in food products, greater product reliability and an application of western electronics to engineering and better designs in clothing. However, much improvement was said to arise simply from using western rather than eastern inputs and where east German suppliers were retained by subjecting these to tighter quality controls. The clothing producers now found they had a wider choice of fabric and colour. The furniture makers had superior woods and chipboards. The food processors benefited from natural skins.

(b) Official product standards

The need for engineering firms to adopt DIN standards meant that additional training was needed to enable quality and tolerances to meet the requisite level. Existing eastern European machines could not necessarily manufacture to the DIN standards.

Food firms had been forced to make major changes to reach EC hygiene standards. Production areas had been retiled and sometimes repainted.

Control equipment was needed to guarantee correct temperatures and cooking.

Furniture manufactures, were required, for example, to meet EC norms for chipboard, in particular the proportion of carbonide to formaldehyde was to be reduced by one-third (the DIN standard for air pollution required a reduction by two-thirds).

In miscellaneous trades there were also problems encountered in meeting higher standards than formerly in order to be compatible with DIN requirements.

(c) Innovation

There have been a number of obstacles to successful innovation by the east German firms. Under the planned system the incentive to innovate was often minimal (old style products could usually be guaranteed a market somewhere, moreover the state would usually take any extra income generated by innovations; Ray (1991) argues that the lack of competition blunted the incentive to innovate and indeed also the necessity for innovation in all of the eastern command economies). Capital was scarce so little investment could be devoted to machinery designed to produce inventions. Paradoxically the command regime did not encourage a commitment to longer term R and D. This was largely because few managers or administrators wanted to take the blame for the failures of any risky projects. Official statistics, in so far as these provided a reliable indicator of R and D activity under the DDR, produce the surprising result that the R and D work-force in the east was almost as large as that in the west (121,000 compared to 127,000 in 1980) and the percentage of GDP devoted to R and D was even larger (4.4 per cent to 2.4 per cent). However, the quantity of spending per employee was only 10-30 per cent of the west German level (depending on the method of estimation used).

Under the DDR there were few marketing and service systems to allow the diffusion of what innovations did occur. In certain cases technological activities were hindered because advanced inputs (e.g. Teflon for barbecue grills) could not be imported from the west. This was usually because of the lack of foreign currency. In some cases the COCOM restrictions on the export of western technology with potential military applications had hurt, and the east German firms were forced back on their own ingenuity to "reinvent" these non-available supplies. As a result firms under the DDR had developed a certain ability to imitate as opposed to innovate (Schwarz, 1991).

In a survey of 473 east German manufacturing companies 43 per cent said that they have been involved in either product or process innovations. This compares to 75 per cent in west Germany. Half of the west German companies have been involved in both process and product innovations which compares with only 14 per cent in east Germany (IFO, 1991).

Summary

This chapter has considered the competitive strengths and weaknesses of the firms sampled. Those most likely to survive are companies with strong product positioning especially on western markets prior to unification, and those which have established partnerships or have been taken over by western firms. Nevertheless all require to update the quality of their products in line with present day western standards.

5 Explanations of comparative performance: Machinery

General characteristics of machinery in east Germany

A number of the characteristics of the machine stock were identified and compared with their west German counterparts.

First, those companies sampled which were selling to west German markets prior to unification had already incorporated some modern (though not necessarily the most up to date) machinery in order to attain the required DIN standards. Nevertheless their product reject rate was higher than in west Germany because of the poor quality of material inputs.

Products which had been sold on DDR or other eastern Europe and Soviet Union markets tended to be made in factories with older machinery working to less exact tolerances. The balance of machinery was different from that which would be expected at a western company because investment was not market driven. Investment expenditure was decided by government planners who allocated funds according to their estimation of the importance of the goods being produced. Where plants were accorded a low priority machinery tended to be replaced only when a plant was fully depreciated. In addition, the DDR regime had determined that a certain proportion of machines at engineering plants should be robotic regardless of whether this was justified (in a western sense) or not. In four of the cases visited plants were designated as prestige examples of DDR industrial practice and were accordingly equipped with modern technology. In other cases numerically controlled machine tools were purchased but subsequently linked inefficiently to other production processes.

Cases of inappropriate machinery purchase, particularly with regard to the use of automatic and computerised machinery, were also found in the counterpart firms in Northern Ireland. The main reason for such purchases was the generous level of subsidisation of investment. In the clothing sector the Northern Ireland firms tended to be characterised by a machine stock which in some ways was more advanced technologically than those of their west German counterparts. The highly automatic machines used by the Northern Ireland clothing companies were inflexible and reflected a concentration on long runs of standardised products. This was a production strategy which west German firms had abandoned about 15 years previously because it was vulnerable to price competition from low wage Newly Industrialised Countries (Hitchens, Wagner and Birnie, 1991).

Apart from issues of the appropriateness of machinery purchases, the east German firms had faced problems arising from the fact that they had been largely dependent on western sources to supply modern equipment. Purchases had been administered centrally by the DDR regime which was tightly constrained by shortage of foreign currency. Individual firms were charged very high implicit prices for any western machines they were allocated by the central planners who determined final choices even though they had no production knowledge. This put the firms under pressure to opt for the cheapest possible machine as opposed to that which would best suit their requirements and over time the companies acquired a rag-bag of machines drawn from a large number of suppliers. Such a miscellany of equipment was hard to maintain and the problems of operation were compounded when advanced western machines were modified by east German add-ons, feeding/off-loading devices which tended to push up reject rates and have a detrimental impact on product quality.

Some firms in Northern Ireland are characterised by the most advanced machinery stock found anywhere in the industrial world and notwithstanding the problems of appropriateness noted above were not disadvantaged relative to west German counterparts in terms of numbers of advanced pieces of equipment available per worker (Hitchens, Wagner and Birnie, 1990, 1991). Perhaps surprisingly (in view of other studies which suggest a relatively small east German capital stock; The Independent, 1991, February 2; Wyplosz, 1991) one survey has concluded that east German firms have a higher capital intensity than their west German counterparts (26 per cent higher in 1988; Gorzig and Gornig, 1991). However, this comparison was based on *Ost Mark* prices which often overvalued west German machinery imported to the DDR (sometimes by a factor of four). Moreover, estimation of the comparative scale of the east German capital stock was not adjusted for the inferior quality of much of that machinery. In any case, it was implied that the capital productivity of DDR manufacturing was only about half that of manufacturing in west Germany.

Age of machinery

Comparisons of the capital stock of different western economies have majored on the age of machinery (Rostas, 1948; Anglo-American Council on Productivity, 1950; Bacon and Eltis, 1974; Daly, Hitchens and Wagner, 1985; Prais, 1986). A negative association between machinery age and industrial competitiveness performance might be anticipated.

Machine age by sector for east Germany is shown in Table 5.1 together with comparative figures for matched plants in west Germany and Northern Ireland. Estimates produced by the OECD (1991a) are also included.

Table 5.1
Comparative age of machinery
(per cent of machines)

	Matched Comparisons					
	Under 5 years			Over 10 years		
	EG	WG	NI	EG	WG	NI
Engineering	22	39	17	36	39	48
Clothing	44	57	66	5	8	16
Food	25	56	30	48	13	32
Other	37	57	31	36	24	33
Total sample	32	52	36	31	21	32
OECD results	27	40		50	28	

Note: Sectoral results for the matched comparisons are unweighted averages of the results for individual firms.
Source: OECD (1991a).

The table shows that capital stock is on average older than that in comparable firms in west Germany though it is similar to the average for the counterpart Northern Ireland firms. Gorzig and Gornig (1991) noted that average depreciation for machinery in east Germany was 26 years compared to 18 years in west Germany. (The age of of the machinery actually in use

47

might be even higher than this comparison would suggest given the tendency of some east German firms to keep equipment in use even after it had been fully depreciated; this reflected a common practice throughout the eastern European command economies (Ray, 1991).) Looking at the individual sectors west German plants were younger in all sectors than their east German counterparts. Equipment at the Northern Ireland companies was older on average than that of their west German counterparts though slightly younger than the east German stock of equipment.

Focusing on the age distribution of plants over 10 years, the west German plants are again shown to have the advantage of youth though the proportion over 10 years old is similar to that in east Germany in the case of the engineering and clothing samples. Comparison with Northern Ireland indicate that a similar proportion to east Germany is over 10 years old and in the engineering and miscellaneous trades the Northern Ireland capital stock is older than that in east Germany whilst younger in clothing and food.

A separate analysis was undertaken of those east German firms which were already selling to the west prior to unification. These firms have on average a much higher proportion of younger machines (62 per cent were under 5 years old).

It can be concluded that east Germany during 1945-90 seems to have shared the syndrome of the centrally planned economies whereby investment was accorded a priority in terms of its share in national output (29 per cent compared to only 20 per cent in west Germany; Economist (1990, October 6)) but much of it was wastefully applied. Nevertheless, machinery is clearly substantially older than that found in west German firms (the OECD (1991a) estimated that 20 per cent of the east German capital stock was more than 20 years old compared to only 5 per cent of the capital stock in west Germany). Whilst east German firms in general suffer the problems of an antiquated machine stock the available evidence suggests that machinery is not on average older in Northern Ireland and Great Britain as compared to west Germany (Rostas, 1948; Daly, Hitchens and Wagner, 1985; Prais, 1986). Thus, there is a widespread problem in east Germany of a dearth of up to date equipment (Collier and Siebert, 1991) whilst this problem is much less marked in Northern Ireland (indeed in the sub-sample of Northern Ireland firms which were interviewed in both 1988 and 1991 the proportion of machinery which was aged under five years increased by 2 percentage points, i.e. strong investment was leading to the Northern Ireland machine stock becoming relatively younger).

Level of technology

Table 5.2 shows the percentage of east German companies which were technologically outclassed by their Northern Ireland and west German counterparts. It shows that in 62 per cent and 85 per cent of cases respectively Northern Ireland and west German firms used a level of technology which was higher overall. In two sectors, on average, Northern Ireland firms were also outclassed by their west German counterparts. However, in the remaining two sectors (food and clothing) the technological level of the Northern Ireland sample firms equalled that of the west German counterparts. This testified to high rates of investment in Northern Ireland which have been encouraged by generous subsidisation of capital (Hitchens, Wagner and Birnie, 1990).

Table 5.2
Level of technology
(per cent of cases where east German
machine stock is inferior)

	Compared to NI	Compared to WG
Engineering	60	90
Clothing	100	100
Food	57	57
Miscellaneous & furniture	50*	92
Total sample	62	85

Note: * Principally furniture.

The advantages of western technology included a greater use of computerised numerically controlled machine tools (CNCs). Ray (1991) argues that there are two reasons for emphasising numerically controlled machine tools: machine tools have always been important products of some of the eastern European countries (in 1989 east Germany accounted for almost 7 per cent of world exports of machine tools) and, secondly, machine tools were the medium through which the new microelectronic technique was first adapted to the needs of industry. CNCs were less common amongst the east German sample firms (one per 50 employees) relative to their west German counterparts (one per 41 employees) though the gap was not very large (the representation of CNCs in Northern Ireland engineering firms was found to be relatively high; one per 35 employees). Significantly, amongst the sub-sample of east German plants identified as probable survivors (see above) the representation of CNCs was higher (one per 30 employees).

More generally, the west German firms had the advantage of specialist machines and an ability to work to fine tolerances especially in engineering. Only one plant in east Germany was up to date. In clothing west German and Northern Ireland companies used more electronic add-ons to standard machines, automatic thread cutting, computerised overhead transport systems (these were only observed in Northern Ireland) and specialised automated machines. (Ray (1991) noted the comparatively unmodernised state of the east German textiles industry, e.g. the relatively low use of shuttleless looms.) In food three east German companies had introduced up to date plant and equipment since unification. One east German company in the furniture and miscellaneous trades was a model firm but all other companies were behind in technology and lacked CNCs and linking devices. They used old generations of technology especially in electronics, manufacture of glass bottles and in making optical equipment.

National origin of machines

Forty-seven per cent of east German companies sampled used at least some western equipment. The extent of this use ranged from two food companies which were now fully re-equipped with western machines to the engineering companies which had purchased a small number of CNCs from the west. As has already been noted, one of the reasons why firms had bought western machines under the DDR was to achieve finer tolerances. In some activities, such as cigarette manufacturing, there were no eastern bloc machines made, but the western machines purchased were second hand and were already out-dated when purchased.

Where the machinery was of eastern origin much of it, especially the DDR and Czech made equipment, was mechanically robust though large and less user friendly. Electronic components were poor and tolerances were less fine than their western counterparts. In contrast the west German firms made use of a large proportion of high quality equipment relative to both their Northern Ireland and east German counterparts.

In 56 per cent of cases west German companies used mainly domestic machinery which reflected the strength of the indigenous machine tool industry. Thirty-five per cent of the Northern Ireland firms also used mainly

German machinery compared to only 14 per cent which used machinery built in the UK. Northern Ireland firms were more likely to buy Japanese and American machines than their west German counterparts. This much greater dependence on foreign machinery manufacturers rendered the Northern Ireland firms at a disadvantage in terms of the ease of repair services. The west German companies derived a further productivity advantage from the fact they often co-operated with local machinery suppliers in order to customise equipment to their own requirements (in 40 per cent of cases). In contrast the east German and Northern Ireland firms were more likely to purchase equipment "off the peg".

Machine modifications

While 15 per cent of the Northern Ireland firms and 38 per cent of west German companies had customised their machinery a higher proportion of east German companies did so. They were under greater pressure to manufacture their own add-ons and linking devices and to develop their own machines since foreign exchange constraints had restricted purchases from the west. Two of the engineering firms visited had manufactured robotics.

Unlike their west German counterparts where machine adaptations were innovative and led to productivity improvements, modifications in the east were substitutes for better western technology which could not be purchased. For example the west German companies made their own robotic transport machines, machine feeding devices and linking devices (they did this to a much greater extent than their Northern Ireland counterparts in all sectors except clothing). In east Germany the quality of any add-ons was technically unsophisticated and any robotics which had been made were also liable to frequent breakdowns. As a consequence there was no labour saved since persons needed to be on hand to replace the robotics when these broke down.

The investment in machine stock in east Germany was not driven by the requirement to achieve competitiveness through raising productivity, nor was it the case that machines such as CNCs were the subject of continuous adaptation and improvement. In general technological standards lagged. For example, in two factories the computerised manufacturing systems were based on 1970s systems though improvements were achieved by adding western electronics to machines of DDR origin. This can be contrasted with counterparts in the Northern Ireland clothing sector which had very up to date computers but, given the inflexibility of an unskilled labour force, were not operated successfully.

Maintenance

Before unification the maintenance labour force tended to be large given the need to not only repair machines but also build new ones in-house and manufacture their own replacement parts (substantial stocks of spare parts also had to be held). The age and eastern origin of much of the equipment meant that breakdowns had a higher frequency than in west Germany. The poor standards of the electronic controls represented another problem. At the same time, neither inadequate attention to maintenance nor a lack of skills on the part of operators were significant causes of machinery breakdowns. This contrasts with their Northern Ireland counterparts who had problems with breakdowns but these arose largely from a lack of skills amongst the labour force, e.g. the operators were usually unable to cope with minor machine faults (in the Northern Ireland firms the maintenance workers concentrated on firefighting and breakdown maintenance as opposed to the west German pattern where priority was given to planned maintenance).

Since unification the east German maintenance departments had been cut back though they were still twice as large as those of the west German counterpart firms. The Northern Ireland firms also appear significantly overmanned when the size of their maintenance department is compared with that of the west German counterparts (Table 5.3).

Table 5.3
Maintenance workers
(per cent of total employment)

	EG	WG	NI
All sample sectors	4.3	2.1	3.8

Required investment

Individual companies were asked to estimate their investment needs to meet environmental standards and to upgrade plant, machinery and buildings. In total it was estimated that 128,000 DM (1991 prices) would be required for each job saved. This overall figure is about double that estimated by the *Treuhand* (after excluding the energy and automobile sectors from their calculations; *Die Lage der Weltwirtschaft und der deutschen Wirtschaft Herbstgutachten* (1991)) but similar to the 110,000 DM estimated by *Institut der Deutschen Wirtschaft* (1991, June 20). Predicted investments were lowest in the clothing sector and high and variable in all other sectors.

Table 5.4 Investment required per job saved (per cent of plants)		
Investment in 1,000 DM	Sample plants	Predicted survivors
0-50	50	36
50-100	33	36
> 100	17	28

As the above table indicates those predicted to survive were plants with slightly larger investment requirements per head. This tends to support the finding that those firms with the likelihood of surviving were not substantially better than all the firms in the sample in terms of their age profile of plant. Whilst they had above average stocks of advanced equipment (1 CNC per 36 employees) they had a very similar plant age profile; 32 per cent of equipment under 5 years old and 39 per cent above 10 years old. What was notable was that the likely survivors had much more distinct plans as to how they would invest so as to attain competitive standards.

Stock of pre-unification machinery viable under new market conditions

Given the level of wages existing at the time of the interviews the following proportions of the pre-unification machinery stock were estimated by managers to remain viable. These figures (Table 5.5 (a)) exclude any new machinery purchased since mid 1990. For example two surviving food companies replaced most machinery with new western machines and clothing companies bought second hand on the western market. Part (b) of the table shows the distribution of firms according to the composition of their machine stock between usable and non-usable plant and equipment.

Table 5.5 (a)
Pre-unification machine stock still usable
under 1991 market conditions
(per cent of machine stock)

Food	46
Engineering	56
Clothing	38
Furniture	53
Miscellaneous	56
Total sample	52

Table 5.5 (b)
Distribution of plants according to
per cent of machine stock still usable
(per cent of plants)

	Under 25%	26-50%	more than 50%
Total sample	38	14	48
Survivors	39	8	53

Note: Total sample consisted of 29 plants.

Managers were further asked to estimate what would be the viable proportion of the machine stock if wage parity was attained relative to the west. Thus Table 5.6 (a) indicates that only 28 per cent of the machine stock could in principle be used by a west German company.

Table 5.6 (a)
Estimates of pre-unification machine stock
which would be usable with wage parity
(per cent of machine stock)

Food	22
Engineering	41*
Clothing	18
Furniture	22
Miscellaneous	28
Total sample	28

Note: * Engineering estimates are high in cases where a large proportion of CNC machines are considered usable.

Table 5.6 (b)
Distribution of plants by per cent of machine stock
still usable with wage parity
(per cent of plants)

	Under 25%	26-50%	more than 50%
Total sample	64	13	23
Survivors	53	12	36

Table 5.6 (b) shows that in 64 per cent of cases more than three-quarters of the machine stock will be redundant compared with 38 per cent (Table 5.5 (b)) with wage rates at 60 per cent of the west German level. In contrast, of those firms predicted to survive a larger proportion of their machinery could continue to be used at both a wage level of 60 per cent (as shown in Table 5.5 (b)) and wage parity (Table 5.6 (b)).

Clearly these are broad estimates and they are based on the assumption that firms would continue with the present range of products manufactured. This leaves open the question as to how far any machinery which was specifically adapted to producing products of a DDR vintage could still be used to make western goods.

Summary

This chapter has shown in some detail the comparative shortfall in equipment and technology at the east German companies. While half the machine stock is usable under current conditions this will fall to about one-quarter as soon as wage parity is attained with west Germany. This gives rise to large investment needs at these companies in the sample estimated at 128,000 DM per employee.

Recent estimates for the whole east German economy have reckoned that investment of between 180,000 and 200,000 DM is required per working position (*Institut für Arbeitsmarkt und Berufsforschung der Bundesanstalt für Arbeit*, 1992, August 7). These estimates are based on the assumption that 34 per cent of the existing capital stock can be retained. They further estimate that the total capital expenditure needed to modernise east German industry as a whole so as to attain 80 per cent of the west German productivity level will be 750 billion DM over the period 1992-2000.

It is important to stress how large these capital requirements are relative to both the total size of the east German economy (about 200 billion DM per annum) or even the economy of Germany as a whole (about 2,900 billion DM per annum). In other words the capital requirements of east Germany would be equivalent to payments of around 3 per cent of German GDP annually for the rest of the 1990s. Further perspective on the scale of this required investment is given by estimates that the five economies of central and eastern Europe (i.e.. Poland, Czechoslovakia, Hungary, Romania and Bulgaria) need around $700 billion (i.e. about 1,200 billion DM) of external finance to double their capital/labour ratios within ten years (Begg et al, 1990). The demands of east Germany are likely to limit the extent to which west German capital will be available for the other eastern European economies and conversely those countries are in competition with east Germany to be recipients of capital from other western economies. This raises the prospect of a world-wide capital shortage and high real long-term interest rates (OECD, 1992). At the same time it is important to stress the relatively favourable status enjoyed by east Germany as compared to the other eastern European economies in terms of access to investment funds (Dornbusch and Wolf, 1992).

6 Explanations of comparative performance: Management and labour force

In this chapter a number of characteristics of the labour force are examined including qualifications, training, skills and training needs.

Shop-floor skills

On average twice the number of skilled persons are engaged at the east German plants relative to their west German counterparts. Northern Ireland counterparts had the lowest proportions of skilled persons. Another study covering the entire labour force shows that only 6 per cent of east German employees did not have any vocational or higher qualification while in west Germany this proportion was 16 per cent; Gorzig and Gornig (1991). These figures reflect the compulsory natures of apprenticeships in east Germany whereas in west Germany there is a "voluntary-compulsory" system (though in some cases in the DDR it was sufficient to have been time-served for a long period and this was converted into a certificate). These were generally two year apprenticeships compared with 3/3.5 years in west Germany. And as a consequence the east German skilled worker was more limited in his/her range of competence.

Table 6.1
Percentage of skilled persons on the shop-floor

	EG	WG	NI
Engineering	88	68	36
Clothing	97	48	4
Food	76	23	8
Miscellaneous	90	22	14
Total sample	88	42	14

Note: All sectoral figures are the unweighted averages of individual plants.

Whilst the percentage of those who are skilled and the total years of apprenticeship training indicate that the west German counterparts achieved 75 per cent of the number of training years found in east Germany, and Northern Ireland just 23 per cent, the quality of the training undertaken in west Germany (see below) together with the proportions skilled at the plants suggest that the west German companies outclass their east German counterparts. However, this cannot be assumed to be true of the Northern Ireland plants despite the 3 year apprenticeship served there, because skilled persons form such a small proportion of the labour force. In general most east German skilled persons do not yet possess the advanced technological skills.

Assessment of the quality of skill levels

This lower level of skills has given rise to skilled workers being demoted to realign with the west German hierarchy of skills. For example at one engineering firm 90 per cent of employees were recorded as skilled before unification but this proportion shrank to 65 per cent following demotions (those demoted were paid at a rate two points lower on the pay scale).

However, a number of strengths were noted. First, only the best skills were retained in the slimmed down labour forces. This has since been noted elsewhere for the whole of east German industry (Söstra, 1992). The remainder were placed on short-term working. Second, the apprenticeships covered the classic skills, e.g. in engineering drilling, milling, rotating and welding. In addition workers were well trained in *Handwerk* methods (contrasts can be drawn with the Northern Ireland counterparts; in one firm the workers had failed to calibrate their tools correctly and in another firm the operatives were incapable of reading technical drawings). In maintenance an ability to build, rebuild and improve machines and spare parts was required to a greater extent than in the west (this increased flexibility in terms of mechanical skills). This latter contrasts with the poor ability of their counterparts in the Northern Ireland firms to maintain machinery. These east German strengths provide a base upon which to build up to date skills and techniques.

At the same time, the east German workers were not well trained in hydraulics, new materials or electronics. In addition their experience has been very specialised and low grade (a reflection of the fact that most companies produced long runs of relatively low quality products). They were not trained up to the required DIN standards nor in appropriate work organisation or in data processing. In addition, unlike their west German counterparts they were dependent on much detailed supervision and guidance on the shop-floor (in this they were not dissimilar to the work-forces found in most of the counterpart plants in Northern Ireland).

Higher qualifications of management and labour

We examined the number of higher level qualifications at the matched plants expressed as the percentage of employees with a university level qualification and the percentage having a technical qualification, i.e. a *Fachschule Ingenieur* (equivalent to an HND in Britain). Table 6.2 indicates the relative percentages.

Table 6.2 Higher level qualifications (per cent of total employment)			
	NI	WG	EG
Degrees only	1.0	4.7	5.0
Degrees and technical qualifications together	2.3	11.0	14.4

The following table uses official statistics to compare higher level qualifications in west Germany and the DDR.

Table 6.3 Industrial labour force with higher qualifications, 1988 (per cent of total employment)				
	EG		WG	
	Degrees	Technical qualification	Degrees	Technical qualification
All production industries	7.3	20.6	8.7	16.3
Distribution of qualifications by function				
Production	1.3	20.5	11.8	51.1
R&D	23.0	16.3	43.1	13.6
Management	8.1	2.6	22.7	3.6
Administration	64.0	53.0	12.2	20.7

Source: Gorzig and Gornig (1991).

Both Tables 6.2 and 6.3 show that east German industry employs comparable numbers of individuals with degrees to west Germany and that they employ a higher proportion of persons with technical qualifications. However, Table 6.2 shows that Northern Ireland matched companies employ many fewer individuals with higher qualifications.

However, Table 6.3 shows that the functional distribution of higher qualifications differs between east and west Germany. In west Germany a higher proportion of those with degrees are engaged in production, R and D and management and similarly west German companies would engage more with technical qualifications in production. In contrast more than half those with degrees and or technical qualifications in east Germany are engaged in administration compared with respectively one-eighth and one- fifth in West Germany. The implication of this difference in distribution is that there are fewer graduates in production, R and D and management in east Germany. (The excess number of degrees and higher qualifications in administration had reflected the need to handle the bureaucratic requirements of the central planning regime. The formerly high proportion of degrees in administration is not reflected in the sample comparisons shown in Table 6.3 given that by the time of the visits the heaviest burden of redundancies had already been carried by this function.) Similarly, but to a lesser extent the percentage with technical qualifications is also fewer in each of these categories. Taking the three functions together (i.e. management, R and D and production) the proportion with higher qualifications at the east German plants is still considerably higher than in Northern Ireland sample firms.

Despite these qualifications the ability of east German managers, technicians and engineers to operate in the new market environment will depend in part upon commercial knowledge which is deficient (e.g. awareness of profits and costs). They still lacked flexibility and are not used to taking the initiative or feeling responsibility for decision making. Pre-unification most of the managers interviewed had no connections with west German companies. They had no opportunities to travel except in the east and received no western trade journals. Their knowledge of western technology was therefore restricted. Management was found to be preoccupied with the introduction of data processing systems in, and between, all departments, e.g. warehousing, production and accounting. In fact, they were giving this matter a higher priority than their west German counterparts and to the exclusion of the more urgent requirement of improving their marketing potential. The east German managers were therefore overly orientated towards short term production requirements to the exclusion of longer term considerations as to how production strategy should be upgraded (in this they were similar to some of the Northern Ireland managers who also sometimes assumed that computerised methods per se would make their companies competitive). Icks (1992) confirms these shortcomings in commercial and technical areas. In an extensive poll of west German firms operating in east Germany since unification three-quarters replied that east German managers performed badly, lacked dynamism and were underqualified. Only 18 per cent felt able to retain the east German managers of any plants they had taken control of even after retaining (OECD, 1992).

Table 6.4 gives a breakdown of higher qualifications by sector at sample plants. It indicates that the highest proportions of technically qualified persons were engaged in engineering and miscellaneous trades and the smallest at the less technically demanding clothing plants.

Table 6.4
Sectoral variations in higher qualifications
in east Germany
(per cent of total employment in sample plants)

	Degrees	Technical qualifications
Food	2.1	6.3
Engineering	8.6	14.6
Clothing	1.3	6.2
Furniture	4.0	6.6
Miscellaneous	8.8	12.9

At sample companies two-thirds of managing directors and production managers were qualified with degrees whilst one-fifth had a higher degree. The remainder all had technical qualifications. The principal university qualification at this level was a degree in engineering in 85 per cent of cases.

Motivation

Poor worker motivation was identified as a problem by 38 per cent of the east German companies visited. The main reasons were a low level of capacity utilisation at the firms and a pessimistic view of the future. Many of these firms were still under the control of the *Treuhand*. Those who had been demoted in order to align their pay relative to skills as compared with west German counterparts were also disgruntled (see above) as their relative pay had fallen. Some eastern workers were sceptical as to whether their factories would ever achieve parity with west German productivity. On the other hand, some workers thought that attaining the new production requirements now being set would in itself entitle them to wage bonuses.

Those on short term work were also said to lack any motivation to retrain or seek other employment possibilities. On short-time working the wage level was higher than if the individual was in training. And in addition if retraining was chosen redundancy pay was foregone. One legacy of the planned economy days was the narrowness of pay differentials which also dampened incentives though this was now being changed (before unification university graduates in the DDR were paid on average only 27 per cent above the industrial average whereas in west Germany they received 65 per cent more than the average).

In those companies with west German management it was said that it will take at least a year but probably longer to change work methods. Some problems arose because workers were not willing to work continuously for a full day and to look for work tasks themselves instead of being told what to do next. Accordingly the problems were least and output highest where methods and speed were improved by machines.

Thirty-one per cent of companies, on the other hand, reported good worker motivation. Amongst these were the companies identified as likely to survive and hence workers had higher expectations of prospects. In addition rising unemployment also encouraged worker attitudes.

Changes in overall worker attitudes were reflected in the absenteeism rates recorded. One quarter of Northern Ireland firms reported motivation problems and 31 per cent of west German counterparts; mainly those employing *Gastarbeiter*.

Table 6.5
Rates of absenteeism

	EG		WG	NI
	Before unifi- cation	After unifi- cation		
Food	7	3	7	4
Engineering	5	1	6 (4)	4
Clothing	25	1	6	11
Furniture	7	2	6 (4)[*]	4[*]
Miscellanous	7	2	6 (4)[*]	4[*]
Total sample	10	2	6	6

Notes: Sectoral results are unweighted averages of the results for individual plants. Figures in parentheses for west Germany exclude those plants with substantial numbers of *Gastarbeiter*.
[*] Furniture and miscellaneous trades combined.

Table 6.5 shows that absenteeism had been reduced very substantially in the east German firms to about one-third of the average level indicated for Northern Ireland and west Germany. Current reported levels of turnover were also negligible. This compares with rates of 11 per cent and 8 per cent respectively amongst Northern Ireland and west German firms sampled.

Wage levels

At the time of the visits hourly wage rates as a percentage of their west German counterparts were as shown in Table 6.6. These rates exclude holiday pay, overtime working and differences in the numbers of hours worked and hence do not reflect differences in per capita wage costs in east and west Germany (because of shorter hours and fewer bonuses in the east the convergence between wage levels in the east and west has been lower when measured in per capita as opposed to hourly terms; *Handelsblatt* (1991, July 29)).

From Table 6.6 it can be seen that while hourly wages are at about 60 per cent of the west German level, having risen from 32 per cent at the time of unification, there is some variability depending mainly on industry. The level represents about 80 per cent that of the UK level and hence is comparable with the average Northern Ireland level (Labour Cost Survey, 1990; Ray, 1990). Hourly wage rates are expected to attain parity with those in west Germany by 1993/4. Between the start of 1991 and early 1992 average wages paid at *Treuhand* companies rose from 1,530 DM per month to 2,237 DM per month representing a further closing of the gap (Söstra, 1992).

Table 6.6
Distribution of hourly wage levels
at the time of interview

As per cent of comparable wages in WG	per cent of plants
70	8
65	11
62	37
60	33
< 60	11

Training

In 76 per cent of cases east German companies had taken the following three initiatives (these were of equal importance); co-operation and partnership with west German companies at the managerial level, visits by skilled workers to west German companies and, thirdly, management courses.

(a) Managerial co-operation and partnership

The eastern managers arranged meetings with west German counterparts and visited their factories. This was given freely at first, following unification, but western management is now more wary of potential competition. From this they gained advice about marketing, packaging, technology, training, pricing and costing. These arrangements in a number of cases were made possible as a consequence of a west German initiative seeking to purchase an east German company. In other instances meetings were possible as a result of co-operative agreements; e.g. contracts given for Cut Make and Trim (CMT) in clothing, manufacture of fabricated parts in engineering, also in woodworking contracts with western companies were subcontracted to the east. In all these cases east German management sought and won work in the west.

These meetings also facilitated the possibility of western managers visiting the eastern plants and making suggestions for improvements. For example, in two clothing plants the active co-operation of a west German counterpart seeking a CMT arrangement helped improve productivity by 100 per cent. This was achieved by better work organisation, use of more appropriate machinery (supplied by the west German partner) and training. Overall, advice received from west German management had a significant impact on productivity in all sectors and at a total of at least 18 companies in the sample of east German firms.

(b) Visits by Meister and skilled workers to west German plants

Following from this an important element in the performance improvement of east German companies was training for *Meister* and skilled workers by sending them to west German firms to observe new methods, technology, work pace, work organisation, work study methods, design, quality and finish. Individuals were carefully chosen as well trained and motivated and therefore as those most likely to pass on their observations. The visits by the skilled workers ranged from two weeks to half a year, and from 8 to 12 weeks for a *Meister*. These individuals were then expected to train others at their eastern plant, because without direct observation of west German practice the east German workers, it was claimed, would have found it hard to appreciate the gulf between DDR performance in terms of pace, quality, and finish and that taken for granted in the west German market. Where east German companies had no partnerships with west German companies their options were more restricted. Personnel were sent on manufacturers' courses and to machine exhibitions.

(c) Management courses

East German managers were sent on courses in, for example, business administration, marketing, data processing, costing, accountancy, work study and labour law etc. Many companies had experienced a large number of mistakes in costing and pricing since unification since this proved particularly difficult after unification. The main emphasis before unification had been on the supply of materials and machinery and there had been little concern about labour inputs and the costing of products. Their initial reaction to the new market had often been to pitch their prices either too low or too high. Similarly, they were not used to trying to relate product selling prices to the costs of raw materials. The short courses attended were only an introduction to the breadth of knowledge required to operate successfully (the same applies to courses which provided an introduction to marketing).

Turning to training requirement for the future, all companies recognised the need for further training at all levels. Further training for management is required and also in plant layout, computing and data processing.

(d) Training needs for Meister *and skilled workers*

Similarly it was recognised that *Meister* and skilled workers need further technical training in modern technology especially in electronics, product standards and quality, work methods and maintenance etc. While some of these subjects were entirely new to management and labour in the east in other areas such as electronics and computing their knowledge was said to be decade or more out of date.

Such training requirements were needed to raise standards in the direction of west Germany. Northern Ireland firms were also in need of management and labour force training but of a different kind. In Northern Ireland the shortfall was identified to be one of a lack of technical training amongst managers of a very elementary kind. In this respect their east German counterparts would have superior knowledge while the Northern Ireland labour force would usually have better commercial skills. On the shop floor in Northern Ireland the problem was a lack of numbers of skilled persons rather than the skills of those persons per se. In this respect their east

German counterparts had a numerical advantage over them.

The significant Northern Ireland weakness at the supervisory level was of a different kind from that of east Germany. In east Germany the *Meister* and supervisors had received technical training. Their Northern Ireland counterparts were usually only time served. The Northern Ireland supervisors were however able to exercise authority over the shop-floor. This was often not true in the east German plants during the transition period around unification.

Before unification the *Meister* worked for the workers, e.g. he would supply raw material from the warehouse to the production floor and would be responsible for quality checks and the removal of faults. The *Meister*-worker relationship was the reverse of that in the west because he was ultimately responsible to the work-force. He was also poorly paid (at worst only three-quarters of the pay of a skilled operative while the wage for a west German *Meister* was on average 180 per cent that of a skilled man; Prais and Wagner, 1988). The incentive to become a *Meister* was in order to avoid some of the more physically demanding handicraft tasks (e.g. welding) on the shop-floor and to move to an organisational position. The large number of *Meister* reflected a political decision to further train a particular proportion of the labour force.

Meister training was either by full time study for 2 years over and above that necessary to achieve his skilled workers' certificate or, alternatively, through weekend and evening courses over 3-4 years. Technically they were well qualified within a DDR context but of unknown quality relative to their western counterparts and weak in skills of work organisation and the exercise of authority.

After unification problems were found to arise because the previous *Meister*-worker relationships meant that it was difficult to direct the workers on the shop-floor. In some cases, *Meister* from the DDR period had to be demoted and replaced by technicians or, particularly in the clothing industry, by graduate engineers, this was because of their poor experience in work organisation and cost control.

Summary

This chapter has recorded the comparative qualifications of employees at sample plants. Overall individuals at east German plants are formally well qualified. However, doubts arise as to the suitability of those qualifications for modern manufacturing. What is required is deeper research on the content of courses undertaken by employees in order to show training needs. Recent work by Icks (1992) reveals that east German managers underestimated training and qualifications needs at the managerial level across a wide range of functions, and it is now widely accepted that there are large training deficits at the lower level of these organisations, indeed more than half of all employees are expected to require further training (*Handelsblatt*, 1992, August 8).

7 Other explanatory factors: Environment, premises and business services

This chapter examines a number of aspects relating to the infrastructure of the east German location and the impact of requirements to align with environmental standards operating in the west.

Adjustment to environmental standards

Whilst the companies sampled did not represent the well publicised cases of particularly severe environmental problems (Hughes, 1991), there were a number of cases where investment will be required to reach western standards. In addition many of the firms visited had already closed down some of the most environmentally damaging activities so as to comply with government regulations. For example, a steel producer closed down a whole plant to reduce toxic emissions, similarly the use of a lacquering system was discontinued, and a switch had been made away from the use of poisonous material especially in the woodworking and engineering companies sampled. Machine tool users had stopped dumping cooling and lubricating oil near the factory.

The remaining problems principally concerned air pollution and in all sectors there were firms which were contravening (west) German standards. For example, seven out of the 10 firms sampled in engineering and clothing are required to reduce the smoke pollution from their coal-fired heating systems. Two were considering a switch to oil. All the furniture companies sampled intended to use wood waste for heating and thereby recycle that waste and avoid their current levels of pollution. In all these cases the German government was progressively phasing in the new and stricter western standards into east Germany.

Two companies sampled in the food sector had for long adopted an environmentally friendly system (only recently introduced by their west German counterparts) of recycling bottles and packaging. The necessity before unification to conserve materials was the reason for this innovation. Unfortunately the materials were recycled more often (e.g. up to 60 times with the bottles) than was technically feasible. Thus breakages occurred which reduced productivity (these were aggravated by lack of quality control and standardisation in glass manufacture). Some adjustments had therefore been required post unification.

It is significant that government regulation of pollution standards in relatively low productivity Northern Ireland is less stringent than in the rest of the UK (although much of the existing pollution there is from agriculture rather than industry) and this is similar to the case of the Republic of Ireland where industrial development co-exists with a relatively relaxed attitude to the environment (Cabot, 1985), though of a standard which would be higher than eastern Europe. Even in west Germany with its rigorous adherence to environmental rules has temporarily relaxed the need for east German companies to raise standards to the western level.

Premises

The most significant difference between premises in east and west Germany was size. All factories were too large and, given the low level of current activity, appeared desolate to the visitor.

In 26 per cent of the larger establishments management was able to concentrate production in the modern part of the factory in order to adjust to reduced levels of output and so were at no disadvantage relative to the west German counterparts. In the remaining 74 per cent factories could not be easily adapted to western standards either because of size (a problem in three-fifths of these cases) or age (in two-fifths of these cases). However, in the case of the smaller firms visited all but one of these were housed in suitable premises. Fifty-five per cent of all factories visited had been established before the Second World War though in many cases piecemeal additions had since been made. Production remained dislocated by modern standards.

During the DDR period large quantities of machine spare parts were warehoused and even inappropriate parts were kept since it was sometimes possible to barter these with other companies (this practice was reported

70

amongst the engineering and furniture firms). On the other hand, under the central planning regime the factories had generally not kept stocks of finished goods. Now they were part of a market economy and demand was more uncertain and variable the furniture companies had found they had to build warehousing facilities. The food companies had to build stores which met the new hygienic standards.

A number of factories were arranging to either sell or rent parts of their premises. Sometimes this was in conjunction with schemes to set up small businesses on the premises, e.g. in steel, engineering and optical equipment manufacture. Eighty per cent of the companies visited had established the ownership of their estate in their own right and were therefore able to sell if required, the remainder were claimed by westerners.

Where larger areas of premises have become disused since unification they had become dilapidated and untidy because of neglect. Repairs and repainting are necessary. Nevertheless the production areas were up to the standards of tidiness of the west German counterpart and were generally much more orderly than the Northern Ireland firms. However, very few factories in Northern Ireland or west Germany reported that their premises were unsuitable for present production though as many as 44 per cent of the west German and 25 per cent of the Northern Ireland premises dated from before the Second World War.

Communications

At the time of the interviews companies in east Germany found physical infrastructure hindered industrial activity. Roads were poorly surfaced and inadequate for the level of traffic experienced since unification. Given that the telephone system was poorly developed and unreliable many firms attempted to carry on business using radio telephones and difficulties had been encountered with fax and postal services. Hotels were scarce and expensive relative to the quality of what was available. This made it difficult to accommodate personnel from west Germany. Many of these infrastructural shortcomings are now rapidly being improved.

Quality of business services

Another locational disadvantage arises from the lack of availability of business services. This section examines some aspects of the demand for and supply of services in the region.

Table 7.1 shows the types of business services which were contrasted in west Berlin and east Germany.

Table 7.1
East and west German producer service companies sampled

	WG	EG
Banks	4	2
Accountants	2	2
Legal	2	0
Management Consultancy	1	0
Market Research	1	0
Graphic Design	1	1
Advertising	0	2
Total sample	11	7

Banks

Bank branches in east Germany were managed at the middle and higher ranks by west Germans whilst the remaining employees were predominantly east German. It has been necessary for the west Germans to train their east German staff given that pre-unification they were involved in only very elementary banking largely concerned with cash dispensing.

All eastern employees were trained, in the cases sampled half were trained to technical (HND) degree standard whilst the remaining half undertook an apprenticeship though not necessarily in banking. In west Germany all would minimally possess an apprenticeship in banking. Those banks which existed before unification were overmanned by two-thirds. East German employees were being sent to the west for retraining on a rotating basis (OECD (1991b) noted the need for additional know-how in eastern European banks). The western managers sent to the east are as well qualified as their western counterparts with A-level equivalents and additional banking training. In principle these western managers can be viewed as though they have received accelerated promotion in the west and hence their experience can be viewed in the same light. They expect a rapid growth of branch banking.

Banks are cautious in lending to firms in the former DDR because of the perceived risk and difficulties in assessing that risk. Problems of misperception of risk are partly a function of the continued impact of GEMU and also because of a lack of information about the financial performance of companies in east Germany (it has not usually been possible to obtain business references). East German bank branches also lacked those secondary sources which in the west act to assess risk, e.g. advice from the Chambers of Commerce, performance indicators such as from DATEV, and local management consultants. They have yet to build up a portfolio of clients of their own with which to compare performance. They fear the lack of business administration experience amongst the managers in east German firms (other commentators have noted that west German bankers sometimes regard the east Germans as naive in their attitudes to credit, i.e. they tend to ask for a loan which is far too big or far too small; Financial Times (1991, February 9/10)). In this respect they would be more likely to lend to a comparable project in west Germany. It is easier to finance joint ventures because of the availability of collateral and a known performance of the western partner.

Whilst the range of services is normally comparable with the west the great lack of expertise, and the training required by the employees to raise the standards has given rise to many complaints from the manufacturing clients interviewed in addition to their difficulties in raising required loans. On the other hand a number of positive remarks about business advice were made by clients dealing directly with western trained personnel. Problems could be avoided by using banks in west Germany or west Berlin and many of the firms were in fact doing this.

The eastern banking branches visited were more willing to lend to such service activities as medical doctors, dentists and restaurants for which a less risky future and more likely collateral would be foreseen.

Accountants and lawyers

Like the banks, accountancy and legal firms in east Germany are led by individuals qualified in their profession in the west. Most west Berlin accountants and lawyers also provided a service to eastern clients and those interviewed had many on the books. Eastern practices employed east German persons (this was claimed to be an advantage when dealing with east German clients). These were persons usually qualified with a socialist economics background to A-level or degree standard. The first difficulty encountered is that most of the detailed professional knowledge lies with the partners and therefore much supervision and training is required. The employees are relatively slow because they are new to the work. Training is required in the use of new technology both to speed up data processing on the part of the accountants themselves and also to provide advice to clients on the appropriate systems they might buy. Training is also required in accounting (including tax) and law. The small firms interviewed in the east have grown five fold in a year and expect continued rapid expansion, and accounting firms in west Berlin have also experienced the increased demand from east German companies. The latter have also employed east German individuals who require one to two years further training to raise them to west German standards. Motivation in all cases was reported very good (pay and job security were above average for east Germany). A difficulty reported by east German practices was a lack of locally available training for employees who would in the immediate future have to learn on correspondence courses.

The scale of fee is the same for both east and west German clients since these are regulated, although the east German accountants charged clients at the lower end of the appropriate scale. The competitive advantage claimed by east German practices was simply, a locational advantage given that the service they provided was that of a generalist relative to their west Berlin counterparts. In addition the east German accountants interviewed unlike their counterparts in Berlin employed no lawyers in-house though they had established close co-operation with commercial lawyers. Their stated disadvantages were related to the weaknesses of the east German infrastructure (e.g. telephones, fax and data processing systems).

Difficulties were encountered with eastern clients especially concerning their lack of commercial knowledge, lack of a knowledge of the west, in some cases a rigid and risk averse approach to business, and an uncertainty of the type and quality of consultancy service which they required. East German clients were also very wary of the scale of fees appropriate to the services offered, where the usual full service (by west German standards) was required with necessary proactive advice, the clients tended to undervalue this. The speed of growth of these accountancy firms also curtails the time available to deal with existing clients given the numbers of trained personnel available.

Advertising and graphic design

Visits to two companies representing these business services in east Germany indicated lower levels of turnover per head (one-quarter that of their west German counterparts) and also a narrower range of service provision though of a more general kind. Wages paid in the east were 50 per cent lower than their west German counterparts.

The advertising and graphic design companies interviewed were managed by east German persons. Whilst all individuals at the eastern companies were minimally skilled fewer were university graduates compared with their west German counterparts. Motivation differed among the east German companies visited according to whether the firm was a new start-up reporting good motivation or an existing formerly socialist company where motivation was said to be poor (this company remained with the *Treuhand* and its future is uncertain; it was weakened when two employees left to start their own business). All equipment was up to date, renewed where necessary since unification but not of as high a standard of quality and flexibility as that found in west Berlin. East German equipment is satisfactory for the simple work undertaken at present but is unlikely to be satisfactory for the future. Premises occupied in the east paid rents which were only a small fraction of those in west Berlin.

Prices charged in east Germany were on average half those of the west German firms and were up to two-thirds cheaper. Both companies served west German clients. These were won with difficulty and contracts were entered at a very low price in order to show their level of professionalism. The west Berlin company also served east German clients who were charged at west German rates. There was little difference between the east and west German companies in the extent to which a single principal customer generated turnover. On average the eastern companies served a much more local market and they were more likely to emphasise communication problems in reaching more distant customers than were their western counterparts even in reaching distant east German clients. All used the same marketing techniques.

Growth constraints differed between east and west Germany. East German companies emphasised finance whilst their west German counterparts stressed capacity and difficulties attracting sufficiently highly qualified personnel. With the exception of the formerly socialist company the other two emphasised quality as their competitive advantage, but both east German companies placed price as the most important criterion for competition over quality, whilst their west German counterparts placed quality first. This reflected the lack of sophistication of east German clients and a high price elasticity of demand on their part. Interestingly neither east German company sought growth as a key objective of the firm. This contrasted with their west German counterparts. The east German companies complained that services bought from the former DDR, e.g. photography, print etc., were of poor quality and delivery.

Management consultancy and market research

No indigenous management consultant or market research agencies were used in the east. Two were visited in west Berlin. These provided a wide range of services. Both had served mainly medium sized east German clients, these comprised one-fifth of the management consultant's turnover and had formerly represented up to two-fifths that of the market research company. The management consultant explained that when selecting suitable clients for the east and discussing their problems much time was required in explaining basic free market economics, and this was a barrier to offering anything above a very simple service. The market research company had difficulty with east German clients particularly with regard to payment (they have now stopped serving clients from east Germany). Market research in the east was found to be difficult because of the poor infrastructure.

In general business services other than accounting and banking services can be supplied at a distance, hence from a supply-side point of view east German manufacturing companies are not at a disadvantage with regard to their location with respect to these services. However the demand for business services amongst sample companies is only a fraction of that used by western manufacturing counterparts and those services which are used tend to be unsophisticated. The local need for banking and accounting services is likely, however, to place firms in east Germany, at present, at a disadvantage.

Use of business services

Firms were asked to itemise business services used during the last year. All companies talked with their bank managers, usually a local manager but one trained in the west, and all received accountancy advice taken entirely from western firms. All the firms received management consultants reports initiated by the *Treuhand*.

All firms considered advice given by banks and accountants useful. The service received by banks as far as financial transfers and transactions are concerned were considered slow and of poor quality because east German employees were poorly trained. This was made worse because of a difficulty of knowing how to make full use of the bank or what regulations applied, e.g. freedom to choose banks (the problems of east German firms have in dealing with west German laws are described by Fritsch, Wagner and Eckhardt (1991)). Their connection with west German accountants arose principally through the legal requirement for DM accounting balances for the purposes of trading.

76

Very little use of other business services has been made (with the exception of business courses and seminars; see below). The average use of any other services during the year was one per firm. One-third of these concerned design, principally graphic design, and the remainder production and technology related to solve specific problems and, in a minority of cases, computer advice. Very little had been spent on these services. While most of these were provided by west German companies, some design, both graphic and product was eastern, and also, in one instance, advertising too. For example, use was made of the MODE institute of the former DDR by clothing firms.

Consultancy was said to be too expensive and too general in type. No criticism was levelled at any service purchased but neither were they able to quantify the impact of those services on business performance and will need to develop rules of thumb for their appropriate use.

Summary

This chapter has shown that the physical and business infrastructure in east Germany is weak and falls short of west German standards. Changes are being made rapidly and many of these constraints are now being eased. For example, the west German utility *Telekom* is not the largest industrial investor in east Germany and the *Treuhand* has recognised the acute need for business advice. A recent initiative has been to offer professional consultancy services by Roland, Berger and Partners for those companies wishing to engage in management buy-outs or undertake start-ups (*Die Berliner*, 1992, June 26).

8 Policy and the competitiveness of east Germany: Comparisons with western and eastern Europe

Introduction

In this chapter the economic performance of east Germany and the appropriate policy response is considered with reference to another peripheral region of the EC, namely Northern Ireland and the other economies of eastern Europe. In comparing Northern Ireland and east Germany the purpose is mainly to establish some lessons for east Germany from the experience of Northern Ireland where industrial policy has been operated for more than three decades. On the other hand, to the extent that superior growth potential can be identified in east Germany, it may also be possible to trace some lessons for Northern Ireland coming from the east German example. Given the speed with which GEMU has been implemented east Germany can be considered as being one step ahead of the other eastern European economies in terms of the process of transition to a market economy and as such may provide an example which would be instructive to other eastern European policy makers.

Comparison of the economic performance of Northern Ireland and east Germany: The speed of convergence

Comparisons between Northern Ireland and east Germany are of particular interest since each has been characterised by generally unsuccessful economic performance for a considerable number of years. As a planned economy during the period 1945-90 the east German economy was subject to state direction while Northern Ireland has developed as a mixed economy with substantial state sectors coexisting alongside relatively free markets. Northern Ireland is distinguished from other western economies by a high degree of state intervention (during the early 1980s state expenditure contributed about 70 per cent of the total regional gross domestic product of Northern Ireland which positioned Northern Ireland closer to the planned economies such as east Germany than market economies such as Japan and the USA in its extent of dependence on public spending).

Hitherto both east Germany and Northern Ireland have been regions characterised by relatively low levels of per capita income. Since the partition of Ireland in 1921 Northern Ireland has somewhat improved its standing relative to the rest of the UK (GDP per capita levels increasing from 60 per cent of the UK average in 1924 to about 75 per cent in the late 1980s) and the Republic of Ireland has also displayed some convergence towards the UK level, albeit to a lesser extent (from about 60 per cent of the UK average in the early 1920s to about 65 per cent in the late 1980s). Yet the gaps remain substantial and during the course of this 70 year period the UK was itself declining from its previous status as one of Europe's and indeed the world's richest economies. By implication, both parts of Ireland were slipping down the European rankings over this long period (Lee, 1990).

The two regions are also areas with relatively high rates of unemployment. For example, Northern Ireland has always had an unemployment rate which is substantially higher than the average for the UK as a whole. The rate currently stands at about 15 per cent of the labour force and is expected to continue to do so. Rates in the Republic of Ireland have varied, in some periods they have been both below and above those in Northern Ireland. In recent years they have exceeded those in Northern Ireland.

During the era of the planned economy unemployment appeared to be negligible in east Germany. After the shock of the onset of GEMU the rate rose rapidly to about 12 per cent by the end of 1991 (the Federal Employment Office estimate the January 1992 rate as nearly 17 per cent, the basis for calculating unemployment having changed; previously 8.8 million people were considered capable of gainful employment but this was lowered to 7.9 million). However, the true extent of the underemployment of the east German work-force is even greater given that considerable numbers of employees who are still on short-time working schemes. (The number of unemployed in east Germany was 1,038,000 in December 1991 with a further 1,035,000 on short-time work, a total of 2.9 million jobs having been lost during 1990-91; training schemes financed by the Federal authorities absorbed some of those who would otherwise have become unemployed: *Institut der Deutschen Wirtschaft* (1992)).

If east Germany is able to achieve rapid economic convergence with west Germany within the next 5-15 years this would represent a model from which Northern Ireland and other low productivity regions of the EC might be expected to learn. Siebert (1991a) argues that both economic theory and the early post-war economic history of west Germany points to the potential for a rapid rate of convergence given that east German growth could be accelerated by the high rates of investment necessary to raise the currently low capital-labour ratio. He expresses concern however lest the special features of German monetary and economic union, such as the extent to which labour costs have outstripped productivity improvement, will mean that much of that potential fails to materialise (Siebert, 1991b). Nevertheless Barro and Sala-i-Martin (1991) have estimated 35 years for a removal of just half of the gap while Dornbusch and Wolf (1992) postulate a dramatic narrowing in fifteen years.

The pessimism of Barro and Sala-i-Martin (1991) is based on observation of a large amount of cross-sectional data which reveals that inter-regional or international growth differentials are typically small and diminish as the gaps between areas narrow. The following relationship has been indicated;

$$g_t = -b \ln (Y_{t-1}/Y^*_{t-1}),$$

where:

g : The region's growth advantage
Y : GDP per capita of the region
Y*: GDP per capita of the benchmark region

and b has a value of 0.02.

Given that east Germany is starting from a level of GDP per capita about one-third of the west Germany then the specification of Barro and Sala-i-Martin (1991) would imply that east Germany would initially grow at a rate 2 percentage points higher than west Germany. This relatively slow speed of convergence would not promote any revolutionary change in east Germany's relative position and the implication is that the growth advantage would taper off as Y/Y^* increased. In short, full convergence with west Germany could take the better part of one century.

These forecasts of Barro and Sala-i-Martin (1991) are based on the application of a generally observed growth relationship and therefore exclude by assumption the possibility that east Germany could be a special case. However, Barro (1991) argued that even if there was an investment boom in east Germany which increased the the investment/GDP ratio by 20 percentage points this would increase the annual growth rate by only 1.3 percentage points given past growth relationships. It should also noted that even the most successful post-war economies such as west Germany, Hong Kong, Japan, South Korea, Singapore and Taiwan have achieved rates of convergence relative to the US level which are at best 16 per cent per decade (Dornbusch and Wolf, 1992). If east Germany simply matched this rate of progress then 30 years from now GDP per employee would only be 80 per cent of the west German level.

There are however strong reasons to believe that east Germany is indeed a special case and should be able to sustain a rate of convergence much higher than the most successful post-war economies (Dornbusch and Wolf, 1992). A high rate of capital accumulation would be facilitated by access to west German savings and generous subsidisation of investment. Rapid growth of total factor productivity might be expected given the elimination of the X-inefficiency inherited from the command economy and the establishment of a west German institutional framework.

One of the purposes of this chapter is to use our own survey evidence to evaluate whether the pessimism of Barro and Sala-i-Martin (1991) or optimism of Dornbusch and Wolf (1992) is most likely to be valid. However, before consideration of this topic the explanations of previously poor competitive performance in east Germany and Northern Ireland will be outlined and contrasted.

Sources of the poor competitiveness of Northern Ireland and east Germany

The two areas share the common characteristic of longstanding deficiencies in economic performance. In each case the underlying explanation of these deficiencies is a lack of economic competitiveness which is demonstrated by comparatively low levels of value added per employee which in turn derive from low levels of physical productivity (i.e. the volume and efficiency of output) and the inferior quality of products. The low standards of east German firms with respect to physical productivity and product quality have been demonstrated in this study and earlier matched plant comparisons revealed the deficiencies of smaller and larger firms in Northern Ireland (Hitchens and O'Farrell, 1987; Hitchens, Wagner and Birnie, 1990).

The substandard competitiveness of the companies is then followed by a low rate of growth and an inability to fully employ the potential labour force. However, it is important to note that the reasons for that lack of competitiveness differ between the two areas and comparisons can highlight the various causal factors.

82

(1) Innovation Northern Ireland and east Germany do share a weakness with regard to their ability to generate innovations and to absorb technological developments originating from other areas. In fact the rate of R and D spending by industry in Northern Ireland lags behind that in Great Britain itself one of the laggards of the western industrial world (Patel and Pavitt, 1987; Hitchens, Wagner and Birnie, 1990). It is also known that the output of innovations per unit of output from Northern Ireland manufacturing is relatively low compared to all other UK regions (Harris, 1988).

There is no doubt that during the planning period the average quality of east German products lagged increasingly relative to those being produced by the western economies. One indicator of this was that the unit price of east German exports dropped (Economist, 1988, July 30). There was a heavy dependence on eastern European markets which were generally less demanding and where products were sold to western European markets it was often necessary for the DDR authorities to subsidise the price to an artificially low level. The DDR has a low rate of output of innovation as measured by patent statistics (Ray (1991) and see below).

(2) Capital A contrast can be discerned between east Germany and Northern Ireland when the role of capital stock is considered. The available indicators suggest that firms in Northern Ireland are usually relatively well equipped with regard to machinery. For example the investment rate in Northern Ireland manufacturing has exceeded that in Great Britain since the mid-1960s (Hitchens, Wagner and Birnie, 1990) and the available estimates of capital stock imply that the capital intensity of Northern Ireland industry may even be higher than that of Great Britain (Harris, 1983).

In contrast, these matched comparisons indicate the extent to which the capital stock in east Germany is comparatively old and technologically out of date relative to west Germany and also Northern Ireland. Only a minority of the machines in east Germany are likely to be usable under the new market conditions (and this proportion will drop as wage costs in east Germany converge towards those in west Germany, unfortunately wage parity would also require a much higher capital intensity in east German manufacturing in order to warrant these higher payments through the attainment of higher levels of productivity; Lipschitz and McDonald, 1990).

(3) Skills and training of labour Whilst the greatest deficiency of east German manufacturing is in respect to the capital stock, the greatest weakness of the companies in Northern Ireland may be related to the quality of the labour force. This is in spite of the fact that the Northern Ireland

education system achieves impressive performances with those of above average academic abilities. Unfortunately, outmigration acts to ensure that some of the most talented do not remain within the local labour market (Hitchens, Wagner and Birnie, 1990). Northern Ireland shares the general weakness of the British education system with regard to its inadequate attention to technical and vocational training and education especially for those of 16-18 years old. In-company training appears to be inadequate.

In contrast the east German industrial labour force is much better qualified in a technical sense such that in 1989 almost 90 per cent had either an apprenticeship, *Meister*, technical or degree-level qualification. This rate of qualification is more than twice that found in Northern Ireland or indeed the UK as a whole. In 1989 5.3 per cent of the industrial labour force were graduates which is higher than the representation in Northern Ireland (if anything, east German manufacturing prior to GEMU may have been employing more graduates than it needed given the lack of sophistication of both products and processes; Burda (1991)). The high levels of training in east Germany were the product of both the traditional German apprenticeship system and the application of the compulsion of the command regime. Whilst, the east German graduates, technicians and apprenticeships would lag their west German counterparts in respect of electronic and advanced technical skills they display high standards of competence with regard to basic engineering, mechanics and the standard operations and they are likely to be superior to the Northern Ireland shop-floor workers in these basic tasks. Moreover, the east Germans unlike their counterparts in Northern Ireland have much more scope to learn quickly from west German best practice, e.g. through sending personnel to west German factories to observe higher productivity work organisation and techniques.

Economic dynamics in Northern Ireland and east Germany

Having considered the similarities and contrasts in terms of performance and policy it is also worth considering which area has the greatest potential for dynamic improvement and economic convergence with west Germany.

An important point to stress is that a substantial gap between average living standards in west Germany and those in Northern Ireland (and also the Republic of Ireland) has now been maintained for at least three decades, i.e. the Northern Ireland and Republic of Ireland economies have yet to demonstrate a dynamic ability to catch up with west Germany (even by the standards of the slow rate of inter-regional convergence which Barro and Sala-i-Martin (1991) posit as the norm within market economies the performance of the two Irish economies has been disappointing). The issue

84

for debate is whether east Germany is going to perform any better and hence disproof some of the more pessimistic conjectures which have already been outlined. The following points can be made:

East Germany is catching up rapidly on Northern Ireland in productivity terms

When levels of productivity in manufacturing are considered it is true that the Northern Ireland-west German productivity gap has narrowed during the last decade though this was largely the result of the relative growth achieved during the years of the so-called productivity miracle of the 1980s and it is unclear whether this improvement will be maintained (Hitchens, Wagner and Birnie, 1990). The following table illustrates the performance of east German manufacturing relative to that in Northern Ireland as implied by the results of this sample study.

Table 8.1 Comparative physical productivity in east Germany and Northern Ireland (as per cent of level in west Germany, WG=100)		
EG/WG mid 1991	NI/WG 1988	NI/WG mid 1991*
Food	60	53	53
Engineering	64	40	42
Clothing	50	75	76
Furniture	63	50	52
Miscellaneous	58	57	61

Note: * Northern Ireland/WG sample comparative productivity was originally measured in 1988 and updated to 1991 using data supplied by sample firms during re-visits.

The most notable conclusion to be drawn from this table is how similar the comparative physical productivity of the sample of east German and Northern Ireland firms were when compared to west Germany. In food, furniture and miscellaneous trades performance is comparable. East Germany has a significantly better comparative physical productivity in engineering whereas Northern Ireland records a relatively strong performance in clothing.

A combination of lower quality products in east Germany and lower prices means that the east German performance is less impressive when considered in terms of value added per head. As Table 3.5 showed the actual value added per head of the east German firms in 1991 was about half the level of sample firms in Northern Ireland. However the potential productivity of the east German firms if demand rose to pre-unification levels could be as high as three-quarters of that in Northern Ireland. Moreover, the output and employment projections supplied by the sample east German firms suggests that most of them will attain levels of value added per head comparable to those in Northern Ireland within a couple of years.

East Germany to become another Northern Ireland?

The jury is still out on the issue of whether east Germany is going to have sufficient economic dynamism to achieve economic convergence with the west. Indeed, one of the purposes of the matched plants studies is to elucidate this topic.

There are some negative indications. Industrial output has collapsed since November 1989 to only 30 per cent of its former level. At the same time any advantage arising from relatively cheap labour costs has been rapidly eroded; average annual wages have increased from about 30 per cent of the west German level in November 1989 to more than half (June 1992; Müller, 1992) which implies that parity has already been achieved with the level of wages in the UK and the Republic of Ireland (and east German wages have already overtaken those in Northern Ireland). Even before these wage increases Akerlof, Rose, Yellen and Hessenius (1991) estimated that most east German enterprises would require wage subsidies of 75 per cent in order to make them viable.

Given all this the question has been posed whether Ireland (both Northern Ireland and the Republic of Ireland) represents a model of what east Germany could become as a large region within Germany which is permanently depressed and dependent on subsidisation from the outside. Some commentators have stressed this possibility. "It is easier to think of reasons why East Germany will become Germany's *Mezzogiorno*, with the current levels of transfers, or its Ireland without them, rather than why it will succeed" (Financial Times, 1991, July 1). Or, as Samuel Brittan has put it, "Experience of... UK subsidies to Northern Ireland workers, are hardly encouraging... It is all too easy to envisage large parts of east German industry leading a lingering slum existence on a diet of state aid" (Financial Times, 1991, May 30). Just as Northern Ireland relies on a very large fiscal subvention from Great Britain and the Republic of Ireland on a net transfer, equivalent to 5 per cent of GDP, from the EC, so east Germany is now heavily dependent on public spending financed almost entirely from west German borrowing or tax receipts. Herr Schlesinger, the President of the *Bundesbank*, estimates that transfers now constitute two-thirds of east German GDP (Financial Times, 1991, November 18). Dornbusch and Wolf (1992) indicate a total transfer of 139 DM billion during 1991 compared to a regional output of only about 200 DM billion. One reason why such dependency on outside assistance could become chronic is that it is over five decades since east Germany has experienced the culture of a market economy.[1]

Just as the manufacturing sector in Northern Ireland has been heavily subsidised for at least the last two decades (Harris, 1990; Hitchens, Wagner and Birnie, 1990) so since the onset of GEMU extensive and expensive state aids to industry already exist (Lammers, 1990) in east Germany (the EC has given special permission for assistance to continue at high rates for at least the next three years). R and D is grant aided and investment grants are provided to re-equip, assist start-ups and to promote the achievement of pollution standards. The European Recovery Programme scheme is directed towards start-ups, small and medium sized firms and the business service sectors (it should be stressed that most of the assistance of the new firms sectors takes the form of loans rather than grants, the significance of this is discussed below).

Some commentators have pointed to the danger that high levels of industrial development assistance to east Germany could actually slow down the rate of structural adjustment (*Deutschen Bundestag*, 1991). For example, if the provision of grant assistance is biased to firms already in existence this makes it less likely that there will be new firm start-ups. To the extent that subsidy payments cushion against the effects of low productivity, managerial slack and overmanning then they may blunt the market signal to improve efficiency. Dornbusch and Wolf (1992) have criticised the *Treuhand* for closing down only about 6 per cent of all the firms which have been under its control. It is alleged that many firms which are incapable of adapting to the new market environment are being kept alive artificially and that this is acting as a brake on supply side adjustment.

In fact high levels of non-discretionary industrial support have been blamed as a contributor to Northern Ireland's problem of a chronic productivity gap relative to Great Britain (Hitchens, Wagner and Birnie, 1990, 1991). Northern Ireland may represent a warning to east Germany of what can happen if there are longstanding mistakes in industrial policy (Siebert (1991b) uses the *Mezzogiorno* as an example of the distortions and rent-seeking behaviour promoted by continuous subsidisation of inefficient

87

industry). Given the needs identified by these matched comparisons and the previous experience of Northern Ireland, intervention and assistance in east Germany should be directed towards the upgrading of commercial skills, business services and the capability to be competitive. Such measures would be less likely to produce a dependency amongst east German firms on continuous subsidy. The question of what type of industrial policy should be adopted in east Germany is considered in more detail in the next section.

The justification for policy intervention in east Germany

It is possible to justify extensive industrial policy intervention in east Germany though such policy should be carefully tailored to avoid some of the dependency type problems which have been outlined above.

One of the grounds which justify state intervention is the likelihood that the market will fail in several respects to produce an efficient outcome. This is an argument which has general applicability and has been used by authorities in a number of EC peripheral regions when they argue that policy intervention will in future be restricted to those cases where it is clear the market has failed. For example, in Northern Ireland (DED, 1990; IDB, 1990a, 1990b), in Scotland the so-called "modified market" adopted in the late 1980s which emphasised a more selective and commercial approach, and the emphasis of the authorities in the Republic of Ireland on the creation of indigenous companies which are capable of competing on international markets (Danson, Lloyd and Newland, 1989; Report of the Industrial Policy Review Group, 1992). To the extent that it can be shown markets are likely to fail in east Germany then there is a case for policy intervention.

The need for an industrial and regional policy in east Germany is reinforced by certain features which are unique to that economy. To some extent Germany's problems are not those of markets failing but the difficulties of establishing markets where previously there had been none. There is therefore a justification for intervention over and above that provided by the market failure argument. It is socially desirable that east Germany moves very rapidly from the low level economic equilibrium established under the planned economy. The market left to itself is unlikely to ensure a sufficiently rapid transition.

In considering how an appropriate industrial policy might be designed for east Germany it is possible to identify three types of policy; that designed for new firm start-ups, inward investment and development of the indigenous sector. In each case the scope for policy can be identified using the arguments of market failure and the necessity to achieve a new equilibrium very quickly.

New firm start-ups There are several reasons why policy makers in east Germany should be particularly concerned to promote a high rate of new business start-ups. Vigorous growth among new firms would partly offset the present decline in employment amongst the medium sized and larger firms. Moreover, smaller firms are likely to have higher rates of linkage with the local and regional economy. One legacy of the command economy was the dearth of small firms; in 1987 4.4 per cent of firms employed less than 100 persons compared to 35.9 per cent of firms in west Germany (Collier and Siebert, 1991). The restructuring of the formerly vertically integrated *Kombinate* does at least create the potential for appearance of a large number of small firms under new private management (as of the end of April 1992 the *Treuhand* had 4,800 firms still on its books of which 1,354 had fewer 20 employees). What is unclear is how far this will happen and how far *east* Germans will be able to start-up small manufacturing firms.

It is very probable that the private capital market in Germany will fail to provide the efficient quantity of investment funds for start-ups in the east. For example, as this study has shown a perception of very high risks in east Germany makes the west German bank branches in the east reluctant to lend to the manufacturing sector (the preponderance of small firm start-ups have so far been in the less risky sectors such as retailing, insurance, video rental, and travel agencies). The perceived risk may have been exaggerated because of the lack of supporting informational services in the east in order to assess credit worthiness. At present the public agencies withhold grant support until the private banks have already agreed to make loans to the companies. However, if the failure in the capital market is to be removed the public agencies should move first and hope that the banks will then underwrite the agencies' assessment of credit worthiness. The scale of the unemployment problem in east Germany (1 to 2 million people depending on how unemployment is defined) is also suggestive of the need for state action to promote new companies.

The need for the state to subsidise the provision of start-up capital is reinforced by the effects of the legacy from the DDR economy. Few potential entrepreneurs in east Germany would have been able to accumulate sufficient wealth to be in position to supply this capital themselves.

Northern Ireland already has an agency, the Local Enterprise Development Unit, which attempts to compensate against failure in the capital market by providing grants for start-ups. The rate of new firm formation for the manufacturing sector in Northern Ireland is now about average amongst the regions of the UK (Gudgin, Hart, Fagg, Keegan and D'Arcy, 1989) though the growth in the number of all businesses registered for VAT has lagged the UK average. The industrial development authorities in the Republic of Ireland have been even more successful in raising the rate of business start-up (O'Farrell, 1986). Indeed, the experience of the two parts of Ireland provides a cautionary lesson for east Germany. It is possible for state assistance to bring a large number of small firms into existence but those firms may then fail to keep pace with counterparts in other regions in terms of competitiveness and growth (Hitchens and O'Farrell, 1987, 1988a, 1988b). The quality of start-ups is as important as the quantity. East Germany may be at an advantage in this respect given that the high levels of technical training amongst the former DDR labour force mean that entrepreneurs are likely to be better qualified than their counterparts in Northern Ireland or the Republic of Ireland. In particular, they are much more likely to be able to achieve standards of best practice with regards to product quality (in earlier studies inferior quality was found to be a critical constraint on growth with regards to small firms in Northern Ireland and the Republic of Ireland; O'Farrell and Hitchens, 1989).

Medium and larger sized indigenous firms In addition to promoting as many competitive small firms as possible policy should be concerned to salvage and revive the larger firms which were inherited from the DDR economy.

Left to themselves many of these firms would fail to make the transition to the market economy. This study has indicated the extent to which east German firms lag behind standards of best practice in the west. If this gap is to be closed speedily then there is therefore a need for the state to provide research institutes which would provide the firms with information and advice which was either free or highly subsidised (the importance to the whole of central and eastern Europe of providing networks to facilitate the transfer of knowledge from western Europe has been stressed elsewhere; Commission of the European Communities, 1992).

If provision of this information was left to the market it would be likely to take longer and in the interim a high proportion of east German companies would fail. Moreover, certain business services might not be readily supplied in east Germany given that these were absent during the DDR economy and west German supplier of such services may not find it profitable to move into east Germany (given the relatively small size of the present market for advanced business services in east Germany and uncertainties attached to doing business with east German firms which may not have secure long term futures). State research institutes could draw up inventories of products according to their potential and the east German firms could also be advised as to the suitability and availability of certain skills (the Federal authorities and their agencies would be acting to minimise any market failures which could arise from defects of information in the product, labour or capital markets). Firms could also receive counselling on commercial, marketing and start-up skills.

The east German position reflects the general point that one of the preconditions for the efficient operation of a market economy is that all firms, individuals and governments are well-informed both about the present and the future. It is obvious that such perfection is not in fact achieved and behaviour subject to uncertainty is likely to lead to economic inefficiency (Greenwald and Stiglitz, 1988). Thus in Northern Ireland the agencies (DED, 1990; IDB, 1990a, 1990b) recognise some of the results of informational failure and suggest the purchase of specialised business advice should be subsidised. Yet they fail to recognise that the responsiveness of business managers and policy makers themselves may be critically limited by their available information. For example, the corporate strategies adopted by NI managers may be more conditioned by previous operations rather than those current European strategies which are appropriate to likely market trends (Hitchens, Wagner and Birnie, 1991). Even direct observation of how West German firms are able to achieve higher levels of physical productivity and product quality may not be enough for NI managers who are unable/unwilling to change strategy given their own lack of training and narrow width of experience. Previous research by the authors suggests that the most cost effective way of improving the strategic information available to managers is to engage in a set of international managerial exchanges including visits to the low productivity area from experts based in the high productivity area (Hitchens, Wagner and Birnie, 1990 and 1991). In this respect the companies in east Germany are at an advantage relative to counterparts in Northern Ireland. This study has shown how many of the east German firms were profiting through partnership and exchange of personnel with counterpart firms in west Germany. Moreover, to the extent that the development agencies in east Germany, including the *Treuhand*, have been able to draw on personnel from west Germany as well as east Germany (Economist, 1991, September 14) their competence in advising the firms how to raise standards to those of best practice is likely to be greater than that shown by the personnel of the agencies in Northern Ireland (Hitchens and Birnie, 1991) whose standards of technical expertise are lower (e.g. engineering related qualifications are less well represented).

Apart from a gap in informational standards another area of concern relating to the indigenous firms in east Germany is that of training and labour force skills. It is very likely that market failure exists in relation to company training of the work-force for this raises the productive potential of the labour force but the given firm paying for the training cannot ensure that the newly trained workers will remain sufficiently long at that company for it to gain the return in the form of increased private profitability (Crafts, 1988; DED, 1990). It can therefore be predicted that the free market will provide less than the socially desirable quantity of training. Thus economic theory (Katz and Ziderman, 1990) provides a clear case for government subsidisation of the training process (any such assistance should be tightly monitored so as to ensure that any training receiving public funding is tending to promote either of the aims of improved competitiveness or enhanced economic structure; the links between training and economic performance are traced by Reich, 1988; OECD, 1989; Berryman, 1990).

It should however be stressed that in Germany the apprenticeship system, as operated in both east and west, has acted so as to internalise this externality on the part of the firms. This study suggests there is less need for the state to intervene with respect to training at the basic level. However, public training institutes may be required to provide retraining of managers of a business school type and for higher commercial and technical skills.

In Northern Ireland there is an extensive budget (about £200 million) devoted to the agency charged with improving levels of skills. Unfortunately the Training and Employment Agency (TEA, 1990) is unspecific about how far they will be prepared to subsidise private sector training spending and how they propose to monitor the implementation of any such programmes. This is despite the fact it is very well endowed with resources relative to the new TECs (Training and Employment Councils) in Great Britain (TEA's budget is likely to exceed £200 million compared to total publicly funded training of about £1,700 million in Great Britain of which 90 per cent is allocated to low grade programmes mainly for the unemployed; Economist, 1990, April 21). With regards to basic skills Northern Ireland is starting from a lower base that east Germany and the danger is that public intervention will concentrate job creation schemes for the unemployed which have insufficient training content to rectify this position.

Since demand in east German labour market is unlikely in either the short or medium terms to be able to absorb all of the local supplies of skilled labour there is a strong case for initiatives which will facilitate the mobility of workers within the single labour market of the EC. Peripheral EC regions with comparatively unskilled labour forces, such as Northern Ireland, would benefit from an in-flow of such workers. (A study of small firms in the mid-west region of the Republic of Ireland demonstrated that those companies which had been established by emigrants from central Europe and Germany who arrived in Ireland in the years immediately following the Second World War usually out-performed those started by Irish entrepreneurs; Hitchens and O'Farrell, 1988b.)

Apart from assisting the indigenous firms through subsidising provision of information and training services, the backward state of the machine stock of most companies is suggestive of the value of grant assistance to the purchase of capital goods. Such assistance would be reminiscent of that given to firms under the regional policy operating in Northern Ireland and

Britain during the 1960s-70s (Harris, 1990). The use of capital grants have been subjected to a variety of criticisms. It has been argued that they can lead to a substitution of machinery for manpower in a labour surplus region and are characterised by high degrees of displacement and deadweight so that the cost per additional job created is excessive (though this has been disputed by Moore, Rhodes and Tyler, 1986). Other commentators have traced a tendency for these grants to encourage firms to purchase machinery which is inappropriate (in terms of the type of good being produced or of the level of skills of the operatives). In the case of east Germany the agencies could seek to minimise these difficulties by operating a selective system of grants (i.e. the scale of assistance given could be linked to the extent of anticipated employment gains from the project and how far it was expected to raise the competitive performance of the company in terms of enabling the production of up to date products).

Certain indigenous firms in east Germany, particularly very small ones, might attempt to ensure their survival through operating in an informal or "black" economy (on the importance of the black economy in eastern Europe during the days of the command economy see Marer (1981)). Such firms would be seeking cost competitiveness through avoidance of the burdens of corporate and labour taxes and regulations relating to rates of pay and other labour conditions. Such black economy activities might be considered socially beneficial from the point of view of east Germany to the extent that they generate employment for east Germans (some of whom would remain officially registered as unemployed) and provide consumers with relatively cheap services. However, the longer terms gains arising from a black economy are more dubious given that firms within the informal economy would tend to be locked into a position as low wage, low productivity producers.

Inward investment An appropriate industrial policy in east Germany would therefore promote a high rate of new firm formation by compensating for capital market failure and would seek to revive the fortunes of the larger firms of the former DDR through subsidised provision of information and advanced technical and commercial skills. The third arm of policy relates to the use of inward investment.

As compared to other peripheral regions within the EC, East Germany is privileged by its access to large scale inward investment from west German firms. Northern Ireland has no comparable advantage. Inward investment by west German firms overcomes informational failure in east Germany through widening experience and raising product standards and management and labour technique. In this context the role of the public agencies should continue to encourage such investment and especially those types of firms (i.e. those with substantial representations of advanced skills or a high rate of local sourcing) which are likely to have favourable spin-offs in terms of small business start-ups.

One could conclude this overview of the scope for policy intervention in east Germany by saying that medium and longer term prospect appear much more optimistic than those relating to Northern Ireland. The relatively high representation of basic skills among the labour force makes it more likely that the east German economy will be able to generate a large number of new small firms (e.g. in the precision engineering sector) which will be competitive on national and international markets. If the diffusion of commercial skills can be speeded up through the use of publicly subsidised facilities then east Germany will have a relatively large body of company and plant managers, technicians and supervisors who will be able to manage production so as to meet west German standards of best practice with regards to product quality. (Earlier comparative studies of smaller and larger firms in Northern Ireland demonstrated that their crucial competitive failure related to productivity and product quality which in turn reflected the dearth of technical qualifications amongst those who manage the production process.)

With this large number of well qualified potential managers and the good basis training of the shop-floor labour force (which again contrast to the situation in Northern Ireland) the prospects for small firms and the larger indigenous firms are good. A further very important reason why east Germany is not like the other peripheral regions of the EC is that it has west Germany next door. Large scale inflows of west German capital, personnel and know-how can therefore be expected.

Reason for optimism about east Germany relative to Northern Ireland

In spite of the problems currently being experienced by the east German economy there is reason to be optimistic that it will be relatively successful in making the transition to a market economy and achieving convergence with west Germany. As this study has shown, the underlying supply side potential of the manufacturing sector is superior to that in other problem regions of the EC (such as Northern Ireland).

For example, *some* east German firms are after only a year of GEMU making considerable progress in moving up towards west German productivity standards. The speed of improvement of the underlying productivity performance of survey firms appears to indicate a relatively rate of convergence with west Germany (Alexander, 1992; Dornbusch and Wolf, 1992) as opposed to the more pessimistic outlook thought likely by Barro and Sala-i-Martin (1991). Over several decades very few firms in Northern

94

Ireland and the Republic of Ireland have been successful in achieving this. East German has the considerable advantage of a solid industrial training system which is not found in either the Republic of Ireland and Northern Ireland (nor in the UK as a whole).

Drawing lessons for the eastern European economies

In order to draw lessons which have a wider application throughout the eastern European economies the results of these matched comparisons can be compared with what is known about the performance of industry in Czechoslovakia[2], Hungary, Bulgaria and Poland (Ray, 1991). In all these economies products and processes are relatively backward in technological terms. At the same time, given the unique features of east Germany's absorption into the German economic and monetary union any transfer of lessons to eastern Europe as a whole should only be undertaken with care.

Outdated economic structures

Czechoslovakia was the economy most similar to east Germany given its long tradition of industrial activity and high degree of industrialisation in 1945. Agriculture remains a relatively large sector in all the eastern economies by comparison with the EC countries. The underdevelopment of service activities under the central planning regime is shown by the relatively low representation of these activities in the GDP/GNP of east Germany and the other eastern European countries (Ray, 1991). This is illustrated in Table 8.2.

This structural bias towards heavy industry and away from the development of service activities was associated with the low representation of private enterprise during the period of the command economy. Table 8.3 illustrates the share of private enterprise in total output (net material product). It can be seen that even by eastern European standards east Germany had a relatively low representation of private sector activity (substantially lower than that in either Hungary or Poland).

95

Table 8.2
Structure of employment in the eastern European economies, 1989

	Bul[a]	Czec	Hun	Pol	Rom	Yug	EG
Total employment (millions)	4.5	8.2	4.8	16.9	10.9	9.4	8.5
Manuf. & energy (%)	38.0	37.3	30.4	29.0	38.1	23.6	37.3
Construction (%)	8.3	9.9	7.0	7.8	7.4[c]	7.3	6.6
Agriculture (%)	19.3	11.4	20.0[b]	27.7	28.9[c]	28.7	10.8
Transport & comms. (%)	6.7	6.4	8.3	5.8	6.8[c]	4.7	7.5
Trade & commerce (%)	8.7	9.9	10.8	8.7	5.8[c]	8.9	10.3
Services (%)	18.1	21.4	22.5	18.5	12.5[c]	26.7	21.6

Notes: [a] 1988 data.
[b] Includes water management.
[c] Percentages based on 1985 data.

Legend: Bul : Bulgaria
Czec : Czechoslovakia
Hun : Hungary
Pol : Poland
Rom : Romania
Yug : Yugoslavia
EG   : East Germany

Source: Commission of the European Communities (1992).

Table 8.3
Share of private enterprise in the eastern
European economies, mid 1980s
(output of private forms as a
per cent of total NMP)

Bulgaria	9
Czechoslovakia	3
Hungary	15
Poland	15
Romania	3
USSR	3
East Germany	3
OECD average	70-80

Source: Müller (1992); OECD (1992).

Alongside these common structural characteristics the members of the former Council for Mutual Economic Assistance (CMEA) also share the unenviable distinction that their comparative economic development fell back relative to western Europe during 1945-90.

Relative economic decline

Czechoslovakia was, for example, a relatively rich European economy during the 1930s (Dyba and Svejnar, 1991). Levels of income per head in common price terms were similar to those in Austria or Belgium. Hungary and Poland may have ranked with Finland (Ray, 1991). Half a century later levels of GDP per capita (measured at purchasing power parity) were well under half those in the western European economies and, in the case of Czechoslovakia, Poland and Hungary, between 30 and 40 per cent those in west Germany. In other words, comparative performance in the mid-1990s was broadly similar to that of east Germany though probably less good (UBS, 1989/90; Merkel and Wahl, 1990). Table 8.4 presents the estimated level of GDP per capita in the eastern European economies in purchasing power parity terms.

Table 8.4 Eastern European GDP per capita, 1989 (US $ using purchasing power parity estimates)	
Bulgaria	5,700
Czechoslovakia	7,900
Hungary	6,100
Poland	4,600
Romania	3,400
USSR	6,500
East Germany	8,000[*]
OECD average	15,600

Note: [*] Estimate for 1988. Average of the estimates presented in Commission of the European Communities (1991).

Source: OECD (1992).

Turning to the productivity of the industrial sector alone, this is also a common problem for east Germany and the other eastern European economies. Ray (1991) presents a Czech Academy of Sciences estimate that Czech industrial value added per employee was 30 per that of the west German level in 1985. The Hungarian Academy of Sciences suggested that Hungarian productivity was 40 per cent of the Austrian level in 1989. This would be equivalent to one-third of the west German level if west German productivity was assumed to be 20 per cent higher than in Austria. Such levels of comparative productivity would be very similar to those measured in the east German sample firms. (Estimates of comparative value added per head in the industries of the other CMEA economies are less readily available but output per head in Poland, Bulgaria, Romania and the former USSR would almost certainly be even lower (Ray, 1991).)

Policy differences: Exchange rate, market liberalisation and privatisation

Although sharing similarities of an outdated economic structure and relatively low standards of living and productivity, east Germany and the other eastern economies are contrasted by the use of the exchange rate mechanism (Burda, 1991). The eastern European countries have retained the potential to enhance their trade competitiveness through devaluation though Poland has latterly relied on the exchange rate more as a means to manage domestic inflation and Czechoslovakia has pegged its currency.[3] East Germany has however lost the scope for such a policy since it became part of the GEMU. East Germany therefore has the unique disadvantage and advantage (it can be either depending on how firms react) of monetary union with a market economy. Continued scope to devalue the currency gives policy makers some more room to manoeuvre and they work under conditions of less urgency. At the end of 1990 Hungary and Czechoslovakia were judged to have gone one-half to three-quarters of the way towards fully liberalising their labour, capital and product markets (UBS, 1991) (the extent of liberalisation already achieved in east Germany has been greater given the "big bang" of GEMU in mid 1990). In all of the eastern European economies it is proving difficult to build up a western style capital market more or less from scratch (Hare, 1991).

There have also been marked differences between east Germany, on the one hand, and Hungary, Czechoslovakia and Poland, on the other, in terms of the manner in which the privatisation process has proceeded (Nuti, 1990; Hamar, 1991; Zemplinerova, 1991). Those medium and larger enterprises which have been sold by the *Treuhand* have almost exclusively been bought by west German companies. On the other hand management buy-outs have been much more common in the other eastern European economies (this begs the question whether the management teams of the Polish, Czech and Hungarian companies will be able to attain western standards). More than 1,400 former managers of east German companies have already been fired by the *Treuhand* (Economist, 1991, September 4) (though 400 of these went for political reasons). Of the 3,000 industrial firms sold by the *Treuhand* by July 1991 only 115 were bought be non-German companies. In contrast the scale of inward investment by other western economies has been greater in Hungary (Mann, 1991), most of this taking the form of joint ventures. A further contrast is that the Czechs and Poles propose to experiment with the distribution of share vouchers throughout the population whereas most east Germans have been given no equity participation in their companies. The advantage of the voucher method is one of equity; the whole population has at least the chance to retain an ownership stake it what was notionally the property of the people under the communist regime. Voucher schemes are however difficult to administer and could have unfair results given that small investors are likely to lack information (Commission of the European Communities, 1992). Whilst the *Treuhand* has aimed to privatise as many companies as possible as quickly as possible whilst ensuring the maximisation of surviving employment there is the political issue (Glaziev, 1991) whether enough weight has been given to the representation and participation of the east Germans themselves. It has been reported that many east Germans perceive their current position as being equivalent to being administered as a colony (Financial Times, 1992, February 4).

Policy differences: Innovation and training

The competitive pressures being faced by east German firms now are likely to be faced by firms in Hungary, Czechoslovakia etc. in the near future as those economies attempt to integrate with those of the EC. East Germany given of the abruptness of the introduction of the DM and market economy represents a picture of the situation which will be confronting policy makers in the other eastern economies within 5-10 years. Eastern firms are likely to experience a shake-out of labour in the same way that the east German firms have in the first year of GEMU though the process may take longer. Table 8.5 illustrates the extent to which east Germany is ahead of the other eastern European economies in experiencing an unemployment crisis (this is especially so if the extent of short-time working in east Germany is considered).[4]

Rising unemployment is a reflection of falling output levels (Commission of the European Communities, 1992). During 1990 the central and eastern European countries (including east Germany and Yugoslavia) averaged a decline in GDP of 12 per cent and a fall in industrial output of 16 per cent. The impact was greatest in east Germany where the declines in GDP and industrial production were 22 per cent and 29 per cent respectively but Poland, Romania and Bulgaria were also affected by severe recession (Table 8.6). Hungary and Czechoslovakia were least affected although output was falling in these countries as well.

Table 8.5
Eastern European unemployment rates

	1990 Euromonitor	1990 WIIW	1990 Press	Estimate or forecast
Bulgaria	5.0	<2.0	n.a.	6.0^{1991}
				10.0^{1992}
				11.1^{1993}
Czechoslovakia	10.0	0.7	1.2	$8.0-11.0^{1991}$
Hungary	n.a.	1.7	2.1	n.a.
Poland	10.0-12.0	6.1	7.0	11.7^{1991}
Romania	n.a.	n.a.	2.8	n.a.
Yugoslavia	n.a.	16.0	10.5	n.a.
East Germany	25.0	7.3	7.0	17.5^{1991}

Notes : Euromonitor includes "hidden" unemployment.
WIIW - Vienna Institute for Comparative Economic Studies.
Source: Commission of the European Communities (1992).

Table 8.6
Eastern European recession, 1990

	Decline in real GDP (%)	Decline in real industrial output (%)
Poland	-12	-23
Romania	-10	-20
Bulgaria	-12	-13
Hungary	-5	-5
Czechoslovakia	-3	-4
East Germany	-22	-29

Source: Commission of the European Communities (1992).

The impact of the decline of the markets in the former Soviet Union has already been felt (Czech exports to the USSR fell by 9 per cent in real terms in 1989 and by further 15 per cent in the first half of 1990; Dyba and Svejnar, 1991). Moreover, Czechoslovak enterprises, for example, have been shown to share many of the characteristics of *Kombinate* of east Germany (Collier and Siebert, 1991; Mann, 1991). For example, a high degree of vertical integration (a Czech tractor manufacturer made its own hydraulics, gearboxes, engines and even ball-bearings) (Financial Times, 1989, October 20). Excessively wide product ranges (at one company, compact discs, compact disc players, radios and gramophone players) and top heavy administrations (22,000 civil servants in the furniture industry) have also been observed. Engineering firms lack micro-computers (Financial Times, 1989, September 28). In both Czechoslovakia and Hungary there was, as in the DDR, an under-representation of smaller firms (Mann, 1991).

There may therefore be a need to adopt policies similar to those which are necessary in east Germany. For example, informational failures of the market should be corrected through the public provision of information about skills, usable machinery and the potentiality of product types. Commercial skills should be upgraded and facilities put in place to enable the eastern European companies to access the experience of western European business experts.

As in east Germany there are some glimmers of hope. Some of the eastern economies probably have the potential for considerable technological innovation now that the new market system provides incentives for this activity. Ray (1991) notes evidence of ingenuity even during the previous command economy. For example, the Czech development of shuttleless jet looms. Like the east Germans, firms in these economies often found that they were unable to import western equipment. Necessity became the mother of invention. For example, the Hungarians successfully adapted their traditional brick kilns. Table 8.7 illustrates one measure of the output of R and D activity, patents gained.

Whilst there are a number of possible limitations relating to use of patents as an indicator of technological progress, these results nevertheless suggest that Hungary and Czechoslovakia outperformed east Germany and the Soviet Union (albeit there was a large gulf between all these CMEA countries and western economies).

Table 8.7 Rate of patents in the USA, 1963-87 (no. of patents per million of population of country of origin)	
West Germany	2,104
UK	1,152
Hungary	144
Czechoslovakia	124
East Germany	33
USSR	23

Source: Ray (1991).

During the command economy period Czechoslovakia and Hungary built up specialisms in certain activities within the context of the Soviet bloc trading area (e.g. certain parts of engineering for Czechoslovakia and chemicals in Hungary; Ray (1991)). It remains to be seen how far a comparative advantage was created which will endure under market competition from western Europe. However, some of the eastern European economies do share with east Germany the advantage of having labour forces which are relatively well trained and skills with respect to basic industrial activities. This provides a basis on which to build a modernised economy (Dyba and Svejnar, 1991).

Conclusions: Industrial policy in east Germany, Northern Ireland and eastern Europe

There is a twofold justification for industrial policy in east Germany; to rectify market failure and, secondly, because of the special circumstances of east Germany's transition from a command system. State action could be used to supplement what could otherwise be an insufficient supply of start-up capital, business services or training. These grounds for intervention are quite general but the legacy from the DDR means that there is an even stronger case for public subsidisation of east German entrepreneurs who have limited access to collateral and of east German firms where the capital intensity is relatively low.

The chief lesson to be drawn from the example of Northern Ireland where an industrial policy has been operated for much longer is the need to give all assistance a selective focus (otherwise subsidy payments to firms can become counterproductive to extent that they encourage X-inefficiency (Leibenstein, 1966) rather than dynamic adjustment to market conditions). Waste and dependency amongst assisted firms can be avoided tailoring payments towards the attainment of competitiveness in terms of the quality of product produced by the firms. To the extent that east German firms do make a rapid convergence to west German standards of performance then their example will testify to the importance of human capital (e.g. the high levels of basic skills supplemented by the ability of the east German factories to bring in west German managerial and technical personnel). This would be an example from which Northern Ireland could learn.

Turning to the comparisons between east Germany and eastern Europe it is notable that east Germany is experiencing the same process of transition to the market economy as Hungary, Czechoslovakia, Poland etc. though at a much more rapid rate. Thus there is a sense in which what is happening in east Germany today shows what is likely to happen in the other countries within a couple of years (e.g. the reductions in overmanning and the breakup of highly integrated companies). However, there are also significant differences. East Germany has privileged access to the west German consumer markets and capital markets as well as to funds for industrial and regional policy. The other eastern economies have the disadvantages and advantages of relying more on privatisation with indigenous management teams. As in east Germany basic skills are usually good and performance during the period of the planned economy suggests that at least some of the eastern European economies, especially Hungary and Czechoslovakia, have the potential to display innovation and inventiveness now that the incentives are being provided for these activities.

Notes

1. Apart from these similarities of economic characteristics there also appear to be depressing political similarities between east Germany and Northern Ireland. For example, the extent to which, given "Direct Rule" in Northern Ireland and the discrediting of local political leaders in east Germany, both regions are almost entirely governed by outsiders with little accountability to the local population. East Germany has also shown a propensity to violence though on a lower level and in a different form from that seen in Northern Ireland since 1969.

2.   At the time of writing Czechoslovakia is in the process of breaking up into separate Czech and Slovak Republics.

3.   The extent to which devaluation could improve the competitive position of the eastern European economies has been disputed. If any industry has total revenues less than the value of material inputs then reductions in either the exchange rate or labour cost will fail to improve competitiveness. Industries in such a condition have been dubbed "value subtractors" (McKinnon, 1991). Hughes and Hare (1991) estimate that in the late 1980s 19 per cent of Czechoslovak and 24 per cent of Hungarian output was represented by such industries. To the extent that value subtractors were also highly represented in the DDR economy (the results of Akerlof, Rose, Yellen and Hessenius (1991) would imply that this was the case) then the potential usefulness of the exchange rate instrument would also have been limited in the case of east Germany.

4.   It would be mistake to see east Germany's transition to the market as being ahead in every respect of the rest of eastern Europe. Hungary, for example, has the benefit of a much longer exposure to elements of the market mechanism (from the reforms starting in the 1960s; OECD, 1992). This could imply that if a comparison were made of Hungarian and indigenous east German managers during 1989-91 the former would show greater commercial skills and entrepreneurial drive.

9   Comparisons of east and west Germany and Northern Ireland

Productivity comparisons

An up to date estimate (mid 1991) has been provided of manufacturing productivity in a sample of east German companies. The level of comparative productivity indicated is comparable to that of other eastern European economies being about one-third of the level in west Germany (actual value added per head for the whole sample) whilst being lower than that of a low productivity region within western Europe (Northern Ireland, where levels of value added per employee are 60-70 per cent of those attained by west German manufacturing).

If the east German firms were now working at close to full capacity their level of value added per employee would be close to half that of their west German counterparts (i.e. potential value added per head was 46 per cent of the west German level in mid 1991). The worst comparative performance was recorded by clothing (29 per cent) and the best in food (56 per cent). When the actual value added of the east German firms is considered average productivity was only one-third of that of the west German counterparts (sectoral performances ranged from 27 per cent in clothing to 56 per cent in furniture).

Table 9.1 illustrates the range of comparative productivity performances within the sample of east German companies.

Table 9.1
Distribution of east German sample plants
according to comparative productivity achieved
(per cent of sample plants)

	Comparative productivity		
	more than 60% of WG	50-60% of WG	under 50% of WG
Physical productivity	56	22	22
Potential value added per head	32	31	47
Actual value added per head	19	9	72

At more than half the plants visits estimated physical productivity (i.e. volume of output per worker without making allowance for price and quality differences) is at a level of 60 per cent or more that of west German counterparts. However, only about one-third could potentially achieve more than 60 per cent of west German value added per employee given the value of their products and only about one-fifth were actually achieving that level of productivity.

At the other end of the scale whilst just one-fifth had physical productivity estimated at below 50 per cent that of west Germany, when account is taken of product values this proportion rises to nearly one-half of the sample. Those companies which could be identified as likely long term survivors (see below) had above average physical, potential and actual productivity performance.

It was also possible to track changes in performance during the first year of GEMU. Between mid 1990 and mid 1991 output fell by about one-third and employment by more than one-half. By implication the volume of output per head grew by almost one-half. One of the most notable results to be drawn from this study is that the underlying productivity performance (i.e. concentrating on those production lines which remained in operation throughout June 1990-June 1991 and thereby excluding some of the effects of the sudden decline in orders) of the east German sample firms has on average improved by almost 50 per cent since June 1990. However, the *achieved* value added per head of the east German firms has probably gained much less ground on the west German counterparts once the recession in demand is taken into account (the official statistical sources imply that the actual productivity of east German manufacturing as a whole declined slightly (by 4 per cent) during June 1990-June 1991; DIW (1991a, 1991b).

It was also possible to track changes in performance during the first year of GEMU. Between mid 1990 and mid 1991 output fell by about one-third and employment by more than one-half. By implication the volume of output per head grew by almost one-half.

This estimate of a productivity level currently about one-third that of west German counterparts is consistent with others obtained from survey and statistical studies (IFO, 1991). It should also be stressed that according to the results presented here there has been a marked improvement in the underlying productivity (i.e. in the level of value added per employee which could potentially be achieved if demand expanded so as to remove excess capacity). (Admittedly this sample study does not include those plants which closed down during the early months of GEMU. These plants are likely to have had below average levels of productivity.)

The competitive weaknesses of east German firms

The chief competitive weakness of the east German firms related to their products given that these were generally of a poor quality and were characterised by inferior market positions.

In most cases advanced technology had yet to be applied to products (in almost nine-tenths of cases technology lagged that employed in west Germany and was inferior to that of Northern Ireland in three-fifths of cases). Machinery related problems were also substantial though of secondary importance as compared to the product related factors. For example, if wages continue to converge toward the west German level then barely one-quarter of the pre-unification machine stock will continue to be viable. The technology inherited from the DDR was backward.

Demand was generally depressed given that sales to other eastern European economies had fallen by about one-half and the market in the former USSR had collapsed. There was the further problem that in a number of cases east Germany was now facing direct competition from western Europe in sectors where there is general overcapacity throughout the industrial world. The difficulties which will be entailed in raising the standard of products to western levels range from very serious in the engineering sector where they will be greatest to the food sector where it was easy to identify what changes should be made.

Labour skill and training problems were of lesser significance and basic skills were being successfully updated through partnership and personnel exchanges with west German counterparts. Nevertheless, there remained a lack of commercial skills (this was shown in part by the difficulties encountered by the east German firms in their use of business services, the east German managers often lacked the experience to judge the quality and appropriateness of the services purchased). Finally, premises were usually too large for present production requirements.

It was not possible to draw conclusions about the effect of location in the different *Länder* on performance. The variability in performance in each location was too great and the sample size too small to distinguish location as a factor likely to effect performance and management in no instances claimed location to be a significant disadvantage.

The competitive strengths of east German firms

No obvious comparative advantages were found amongst the sample firms though it is in principle possible to envisage east German firms acquiring a comparative advantage on account of raw material, locational (e.g. closeness to other eastern European markets) or historical (e.g. prolonged experience of a certain industrial activity or technique) grounds. Perhaps some of these comparative advantages will be observed in due course amongst surviving companies which succeed in upgrading their inputs of labour and capital.

One advantage which may not now be worth very much is the experience some of the east German firms had of working in the former Soviet Union. Relatively low wages represent an advantage for the east German firms in terms of cost competitiveness but this is being rapidly eroded (labour costs are already much in excess of those in eastern European economies and are converging rapidly with those in Britain and Northern Ireland).

One ray of hope is that the representation of skilled workers is considerably higher than that found in Britain and Northern Ireland (the proportion of skilled workers on the shop-floor was six times higher). Admittedly, experience of more advanced technologies would be lacking. Moreover, the east German apprenticeship system as operated during 1949-89 lagged behind the west German "dual" system (shorter and less rigorous courses) and it will be some time before east German standards can be raised to the west German level. At the same time east Germany does at least have a general apprenticeship system in place whereas Britain and Northern Ireland continue to suffer from the lack of a general industrial training scheme.

110

Prospects for company survival

The detailed data collected in this study allowed forecasts to be made as to which of the sample firms were most likely to survive. In general, the likely survivors were identified by the relative strength of their products. Conversely, the plants most likely to shut down were those where it was hard to envisage a switch in production towards those types of goods which would be of sufficient quality and sophistication to sell under the new market conditions.

Most of the probable survivors (almost two-thirds) had links with west German partners (either they had been purchased by a west German company or there was co-operation concerning production and/or marketing). The west German companies had themselves evaluated these east German partners as likely to survive.

Conclusions of the study

If the east German economy is to perform satisfactorily in terms of generating socially acceptable levels of employment and living standards it will be necessary for it to develop a tradeables sector which is competitive with the GEMU. Since manufacturing provides the bulk of tradeable goods (and these comparisons suggest that the tradeable services sector in east Germany may be especially weak) then much of the burden of adjustment falls on this sector.

The best indicator of competitiveness is the comparative level of value added per head (increased cost competitiveness can in principle be obtained through depreciation of the exchange rate and by reductions in labour costs but both of these are no longer feasible options for east Germany). Value added is itself derived from physical productivity and product quality. These comparisons suggest that the east German firms have already attained Northern Ireland levels of physical productivity though a substantial gap remains relative to west Germany. Above all else, the long run competitiveness and hence survival of east German firms will be determined by whether they are able to attain the level of product quality reached in the west. One of the encouraging results of this study was that it suggested about half of the sample firms will be able to do this.

Policy implications

In order that as many east German firms as possible can attain west German levels of productivity a number of processes should be continued and encouraged. East German plants should replace top management with those who have experience of the market economy. Upgrading of the machine stock is necessary and should be selectively subsidised. Inward investment and partnership with west German companies and new business start-ups also need to be promoted. Unlike counterparts in Northern Ireland or other EC peripheral regions, the east German plants have been able to acquire senior managerial talent from west Germany. Machine and technological upgrading has been appropriate to the level of mechanical skills of the shop-floor labour force and to future production plans which are viable. Because of these special advantages the long run prospects for the east German manufacturing sector appear to be superior to those for manufacturing in Northern Ireland.

In more detail it is possible to identify three types of policy; that designed for new start-ups, inward investment and the development of the indigenous sector. In each case the scope for policy can be identified using arguments of market failure and the necessity to achieve a new equilibrium with a fuller employment of labour very quickly.

Support for new start-ups

It is very likely that the private capital market in Germany will fail to provide the efficient quantity of investment funds for start-ups in the east. Furthermore perceived risk may be exaggerated because of a lack of information to assess investment proposals and creditworthiness. In addition few potential entrepreneurs in east Germany will have accumulated sufficient wealth to supply capital themselves. For these reasons direct subsidy support should be provided (Albach, Grunert and Schwarz, 1992).

The quality of start-ups is as important as the quantity. East Germany may be at an advantage in this respect given high levels of technical training amongst the former DDR labour force which means that entrepreneurs are likely to be better qualified than for example their counterparts in Northern Ireland or the Republic of Ireland.

Support for medium and larger sized indigenous firms

One difficulty which has affected east German companies is that the privatisation process has been slow. This has created uncertainty for east German management and many reported difficulties (and losses) in entering contracts with customers and suppliers and therefore in making decisions over required investment in capital and labour. Such delays should be avoided.

The evidence assembled in this study suggests that only those companies presently manufacturing products which have achieved strong market positions especially with regard to quality and/or fostered relations with foreign companies are appropriate for selective subsidy. This suggests that the viability of products made by east German firms should be evaluated in order to enable a policy of selective state support to be followed. East German management has little to offer in collateral partly as a consequence of uncertainty over the ownership of assets. Soft loans or grants should be made available for management buy-outs and managerial collaboration with west German or foreign firms. Such a policy of selective financial assistance should be provided with a minimum of uncertainty.

In addition there is a need for the state to provide research institutes which will provide firms with information and advice about products, processes and markets (CEST, 1991) and medium term consulting advice at all levels should be made available to enable companies to draw on the experience on management consultants and others on a continuous basis during the transition period. Such consultancy should be of an appropriate quality.

Another area of concern is that of training and labour force skills. It is very likely that market failure exists in relation to company training of the work-force. Such training requires selective and accountable subsidy of training and the provision of training centres of west German standard. East German firms have been hampered by the requirement to retrain much of their former labour force.

Public training institutes of a business school type may be required to provide retraining of managers for higher commercial and technical skills (Lenske, 1992). In addition a cost effective way of improving information available to managers is to engage in managerial exchanges (Hitchens, Wagner and Birnie, 1991). Many east German firms are profiting through partnership and exchange of personnel with counterpart firms in west Germany.

The backward state of the machine stock of most companies is suggestive of the value of grant aid to purchase capital goods. Agencies should operate a selective system of grants rather than one of automatic assistance (non-selective grant regimes have been criticised in the context of the Irish economies). Assistance should be linked to product competitiveness as well as job creation.

Inward investment

There should be support for inward investment. Inward investment overcomes problems of informational failure through widening experience and raising product standards and introducing new management and labour force techniques. Additionally, to the extent that it promotes favourable spin offs to small businesses and new start-ups it is less likely that a dualistic industrial structure (i.e. a strong externally controlled sector alongside weak indigenous firms) as found in the Republic of Ireland (O'Malley, 1989) will develop in east Germany.

Why an industrial policy should be pursued in east Germany

The burden on the west German exchequer of absorbing the east German economy and in particular of updating the industrial base and infrastructure has proved to be unexpectedly large (transfers to east Germany were equivalent to 5.5 per cent of west German GNP in 1991; Siebert, 1991b). Given this it might be argued that the last thing Germany needs is an expensive industrial or regional policy in eastern *Länder*. These arguments are strengthened by the fear that active industrial policy intervention by the *Treuhand* or any other agency would slow the rate of dynamic adjustment in east Germany (Siebert, 1991b; Dornbusch and Wolf, 1992). The experience of the longstanding regional policies in the UK and especially in Northern Ireland does not appear to present a favourable augury to east Germany. Prolonged subsidisation of industry in Northern Ireland, and especially of capital, has been associated with a chronic productivity gap relative to manufacturing in Great Britain, overmanning and relatively low product quality (Hitchens, Wagner and Birnie, 1990). Nevertheless, there is still a very strong case for industrial policy in east Germany and it is worth restating the main points of this argument which are threefold: market failure, likely effectiveness of policy, and the need to ensure an equitable treatment of the population of the former DDR.

The general justification for industrial or regional policy is that markets sometimes fail to produce efficient or socially desirable outcomes. In fact there is a peculiar east German twist to the usual market failure argument because in this case the state is required not so much to correct market mechanisms which have failed but to substitute for markets which either do not exist at all or else are poorly developed after six decades of a command economy.

The second point is that the Northern Ireland experience does not provide a good model of what are likely to be effects of industrial policy in east Germany. In Northern Ireland high rates of subsidy have cushioned firms

114

against their failure to raise physical productivity and product quality. This under-performance has been associated with low levels of human capital at both the shop-floor and managerial level (Hitchens, Wagner and Birnie, 1990). In east Germany, however, as we have shown here the basic stock of human capital is good. There is therefore the potential for productivity improvement (the new growth theories stress how far rates of economic growth and the speed of convergence with international leaders are correlated with the size of the initial endowment of educated manpower; Barro, 1989). Moreover, consideration of the sample firms illustrates how rapidly they have been able to augment their human capital through importation of west German managers and exchange of other personnel. The underlying productivity performance of the east German sample firms was indicated to have jumped 50 per cent during June 1990- June 1991 such that potential physical productivity was already on a level with their counterparts in Northern Ireland. Thus manufacturing in east Germany has already shown that it is unlikely to relapse into dependency and repeat the experience of firms in Northern Ireland.

Industrial policy in east Germany is therefore justified by failures or absences of markets and it is also likely to prove more effective than the types of intervention which have operated in some of the depressed regions of the market economies. There are also equity grounds for policy to ensure that the population of east Germany is fairly treated. These are especially important given that the purpose of policy should not only be to integrate east Germany into a market economy but also into what the west Germans have termed a *Soziale Marktwirtschaft* (Social Market Economy) (Erhard, 1958; Röpke, 1960). According to the theory of the Social Market Economy social justice is not only a desirable companion to economic efficiency but it is a necessary precondition for successful operation of a market economy.

The first equity consideration is to promote a greater measure of equality of opportunity between east and west Germans. It is unlikely that east Germans would have built-up sufficient private savings during 1949-89 to allow them to now start new businesses (and only some east Germans are going to have their capital augmented by the restitution being provided for the property which was nationalised by the communists). As we have already shown the private capital market (i.e. the west German banks now operating in west Germany) is unlikely to provide funds for potential east German entrepreneurs. Direct grants should therefore be provided to such persons conditional on evaluation of their business plans and the quality of the entrepreneur (the present package of assistance relies too heavily on loans and the use of the commercial banks to provide an initial screening as to who should be eligible for assistance). The aim would be to put the potential new firm founder in Dresden on closer to an equal footing with his/her counterpart in Dortmund. The need for cash grants to entrepreneurs has long been accepted in the Republic of Ireland and the depressed regions of the UK. Admittedly these policies have had mixed results (Gudgin, Hart, Fagg, Keegan and D'Arcy, 1989) and the Republic of Ireland a high rate of new firm formation has been induced but the rate of growth of established firms remains relatively low perhaps because generous assistance has led entrepreneurs of doubtful quality to start firms (O'Farrell, 1986; Hitchens and O'Farrell, 1988b). However, this British and Irish experience is less likely to be repeated in east Germany given the higher level of basic skills.

A second equity consideration is the need to avoid a situation where the control of east German industry passed entirely out of the region. Of the 5000 firms already privatised by the *Treuhand* by the end of 1991 around four-fifths had been taken over by west German companies (a further 233 had overseas buyers and there had been 808 "buy-ins" or "buy-outs") (Mullineux, 1991). The *Treuhand* should now encourage (through selective subsidy and the provision of commercial training for managers) management buy-outs by mainly east German management teams to ensure the survival of a base of "indigenous" companies in east Germany (Müller, 1992). Such a policy should be pursued even if it sometimes conflicts with have hitherto been the stated objectives of the *Treuhand*: to maximise the price for which assets are sold off, and to ensure the highest possible level of continuing employment in surviving firms.

The justification of such a policy is partly the unfavourable experience of regions in western Europe (notably Northern Ireland and the Republic of Ireland) which have relied heavily on inward investment by branch plants and have failed to build up locally owned manufacturing firms (Telesis, 1982; Harris, 1990). The wider social and political justification for such a policy is that it would be extremely undesirable and dangerous if 16 million people felt they had lost all control of their economic destiny.[1]

Lessons for eastern Europe

The competitive pressures being faced by east German firms are likely to be faced by firms in eastern Europe in the near future. Whilst showing similarities of an outdated economic structure and relatively low standards of living and productivity (Ray, 1991), east Germany stands in contrast to other eastern European economies given the abruptness with which east Germany lost the scope to use the exchange rate mechanism. As a result the impact of the change to a market economy in eastern European countries can be expected to be similar to that already felt in east Germany but the effects on output and employment more gradual (Wyplosz, 1991).

116

There may therefore be a need to adopt policies similar to those which are necessary in east Germany. However, there are also significant differences. East Germany has access to large funds for industrial and regional policy and can also more readily tap into the knowledge and skills of a best practice economy (Commission of the European Communities, 1992). The degree of co-operation evidenced in this study between and east and west German firms with an apparently significant impact on company performance could not therefore be expected to be replicated in either quality or quantity in eastern Europe. Budgetary constraints will imply that industrial policy in the eastern European economies will have to be more selective than that operating in east Germany.

The need for follow up research

The main aim of these comparisons was to establish a benchmark to trace change at east German companies following unification and to contrast performance with west Germany and a low productivity market economy; Northern Ireland. The overall purpose is to draw lessons useful to policy both in east Germany and eastern Europe.

It has been possible to trace performance change during the first year of German unification, however much of the value of the work will rest on tracing the development of those eastern firms given their strengths and weaknesses, firms strategies and German industrial and regional support.

At the time of the plant visits only two-fifths of the east German plants had already been privatised. All the east German companies were making plans to achieve long term viability though this study notes that just about one-half of those sampled are likely to survive. The success with which policy is able to address the problems encountered by those firms should be traced for at least five years past unification, i.e. beyond the expected date of wage parity with west Germany. The restructuring required to raise productivity levels will provide a dynamic lesson for policy in eastern Europe.

The advantage of this research technique is that of tracing in detail the factors affecting survival of a cohort of companies visited and interviewed very intensively soon after unification. This will reveal the mechanisms of restructuring as it occurs and in addition enable the plans of management to be compared with the actual outcomes achieved. Failing companies can be resampled in order to retain the sample size. Periodic visits every eighteen months are suggested.

Notes

1. If this did happen it would be especially sad given that the east Germans could argue with some justice that this was the second time in half a century that a heavy burden of economic adjustment had been imposed upon them. During the imposition of communism in the 1940s they missed out on that assistance which west Germany received (food aid and then ultimately the Marshall Plan) to aid the recovery of consumption and investment levels whilst being the only part of Germany to be forced to pay reparations (to the USSR), and now during the transition to the market economy the capital stock which theoretically belonged to the people is being sold off to west German firms at a minimal price.

Bibliography

Akerlof, G.A., Rose, A.K., Yellen, J.L. and Hessenius, H. (1991), "East Germany in from the cold: The economic aftermath of currency union", *Brookings Papers on Economic Activity*, no. 1, pp. 1-87.

Albach, H., Grunert, H. and Schwarz, R. (1992), "*Technologiepotential Brandenburg*", *Discussion Paper*, Science Centre, Berlin.

Alexander, L. (1992), "Comments and discussion" on Dornbusch, R. and Wolf, H., "Economic transition in east Germany", *Brookings Papers on Economic Activity*, 1992 no. 1, pp. 262-68.

Anglo-American Council on Productivity, (1950), *Productivity Team Report on Cotton Spinning*, Anglo-American Council on Productivity, London.

Bacon, R.W. and Eltis, W.A. (1974), "The age of US and UK machinery", *Monograph*, no. 3, National Economic Development Organisation, London.

Barro, R.J. (1991), "Economic growth in a cross-section of countries", *Quarterly Journal of Economics*, no. 106, pp. 407-43.

Barro, R.J. and Sala-i-Martin, X. (1991), "Convergence across states and regions", *Brookings Papers on Economic Activity*, 1991 no. 1, pp. 107-58.

Begg, D., Danthine, J-P, Giavazzi, F. and Wyplosz, C. (1990), "The east, the Deutschmark and EMU", in R. Portes and L. Spaventa (ed), *Monitoring European Integration: The Impact of Eastern Europe*, Centre of Economic Policy Research, London.

Berryman, S.E. (1990), "Training in the United States: The State of Play and Future Possibilities", *Paper presented to Training Policy Seminar*, Oriel College, Oxford, July 18-19.

119

Bode, E. and Krieger-Boden, C. (1990), "*Sektorale Strukturprobleme und regionale Anpassungseffordernisse der Wirtschaft in den neuen Bundeslandern*", Die Weltwirtschaft, Heft 2, pp. 84-97.

Bryson, P.J. and Melzer, M. (1991), *The End of The East German Economy*, Macmillan, London.

Burda, M. (1991), "Labor and product markets in Czechoslovakia and the ex-GDR: A twin study", *Discussion Paper*, no. 78, Centre for Economic Policy Research, London.

Cabot, D. (1985), *The State of the Environment*, An Foras Forbartha, Dublin.

CEST (1991), "Attitudes to innovation in Germany and Britain: A comparison", *Centre for Exploitation of Science and Technology Report*, London.

Collier, I. and Siebert, H. (1991), "The economic integration of post-Wall Germany", *American Economic Review*, vol. 81, no. 2, pp. 196-201.

Commerzbank, (1991), "Privatising eastern Germany: Emerging opportunities for investors", *The Commerzbank Report*, no. 3/91.

Commission of the European Communities (1991), *Panorama of EC Industry 1991-1992*, Office for Official Publications, Luxembourg.

Commission of the European Communities (1992), "Socio-economic situation and development of the regions in the neighbouring countries of the Community in Central and Eastern Europe", *Regional Development Studies*, no. 2.

Crafts, N.F.R. (1988), "British economic growth before and after 1979: A review of the evidence", *Discussion Paper*, no. 292, Centre for Economic Policy Research, London.

Daly, A., Hitchens, D.M.W.N, and Wagner, K. (1985), "Productivity, machinery and skills in a sample of British and German manufacturing plants", *National Institute Economic Review*, no. 111, pp. 48-62.

Danson, M, Lloyd, G and Newlands, D. (1989), "The role of regional development agencies in Economic regeneration: a Scottish case study", *Paper presented to the Development Studies Association Annual Conference*, Belfast (September).

DED, (1990), *Competing in the 1990s: Northern Ireland The key to Growth*, Department of Economic Development, Belfast.

Deutschen Bundestag, (1987), "*Materialen zum Bericht zur Lage der Nation im geteilen Deutschland*", November.

Deutschen Bundestag, (1991), "*Jahresgutachten 1991/92 des Sachverstandigenrates zur Begutachtung der gesamtwirtschaftlichen Entwicklung*", Drucksache, no. 12/1618.

Die Berliner (1992, June 26), *Wirtschaft 13*, no. 13.

DIW, (1990a), *"Wochenbericht 26"*, *Deutsches Institut für Wirtschaftsforschung*.

DIW, (1990b), *"Quantitative Aspekte einer Reform von Wirtschaft und Finanzen in der DDR"*, *Wochenbericht*, no. 17, *Deutsches Institut für Wirtschaftsforschung*.

DIW, (1991a), *"Wochenbericht 12"*, *Deutsches Institut für Wirtschaftsforschung*.

DIW, (1991b), *"Wochenbericht 39-40"*, *Deutsches Institut für Wirtschaftsforschung*.

DIW, (1992), *"Wochenbericht 12-13"*, *Deutsches Institut für Wirtschaftsforschung*.

Dornbusch, R. and Wolf, H. (1992), "Economic Transition in Eastern Germany", *Brookings Papers on Economic Activity*, 1992 no. 1, pp. 235-72.

Dyba, K. and Svejnar, J. (1991), "Czechoslovakia: Recent economic developments and prospects", *American Economic Review*, vol. 81, no. 2, pp. 185-90.

Economist, (1988, July 30), "East Germany's sad miracle".

Economist, 1990, April 21, "The training trap".

Economist, (1990, October 6), "German statistics".

Economist, (1991, January 12), "Post-communist poverty".

Economist, (1991, September 14), "Privatising east Germany".

Economist, (1992, August 29), "Mass appeal".

Erhard, L. (1958), *Prosperity Through Competition*, Allen and Unwin, London.

Filip-Koln, R. and Ludwig, U. (1990), *"Dimensionen eines Ausgleichs des Wirtschaftsgefalles zur DDR"*, *Discussion Paper*, no. 3, *Deutsches Institute für Wirtschaftsforschung*.

Financial Times, (1989, September 11), Exodus from a socialist paradise".

Financial Times, (1989, September 28), "Building to maintain an engineering tradition".

Financial Times, (1989, October 20), "Czech industry grappling with a new autonomy".

Financial Times, (1991, February 9/10), "Renaissance in Dresden".

Financial Times, (1991, May 30), "Capitalist re-entry: A tale of two states".

Financial Times, (1991, July 1), "A nation unified and yet apart".

Financial Times, (1991, November 18), "German economy "to come under IMF fire"".

Financial Times, (1992, February 4), "Germany recoils at Stasimoral snakepit".

Financial Times, (1992, September 9), "Competitive disadvantage of east underlined".

Fritsch, M., Wagner, K. and Eckhardt, C.F. (1991), *"Regionalpolitik im Ostdeutschland, Massnahmen, Implementationsprobleme und erste Ergebnisse"*, *Wirtschaftsdienst*, no. 12, pp. 626-31.

Glaziev, S. (1991), "Transformation of the Soviet economy: Economic reforms and structural crisis", *National Institute Economic Review*, no. 138, pp. 97-108.

Gorzig, B. and Gornig, M. (1991), *Produktivitat und Weftbewerbsfahigkeit der Wirtschaft der DDR*, DIW, Heft 121, Berlin.

Greenwald, B. and Stiglitz, J.E. (1988), "Pareto inefficiency of market economies: search and efficiency wage models", *American Economic Association Papers and Proceedings*, vol. 78, no.2.

Gudgin, G., Hart, M., Fagg, J., Keegan, R., and D'Arcy E. (1989), "Job generation in manufacturing industry 1973-1986: a comparison of Northern Ireland with the Republic of Ireland and the English Midlands", *Northern Ireland Economic Research Centre Report*, Belfast.

Hamar, J. (1991), "The Problems of Privatisation and the Role of joint Ventures in the Transition of the Hungarian Economy", *Paper presented to the Conference of the European Association for Research in Industrial Economics*, September, Ferrara.

Handelsblatt (1992, August 8), *"Ortleb will das "Ohrfeigenprinzip" in der ostdeutschen Weiterbildung abschaffen"*.

Hare, P.G. (1991), "The assessment of microeconomic transition in eastern Europe", *Oxford Review of Economic Policy*, vol. 7, no. 4, pp. 1-16.

Hare, P.G. and Hughes, G. (1991), "Competitiveness and industrial restructuring in Czechoslovakia, Hungary and Poland", *Discussion Paper Series*, no. 543, Centre for Economic Policy Research, London.

Harris, R.I.D. (1983), "The measurement of capital services in production for the UK regions 1968-78", *Regional Studies*, vol. 17, no. 3, pp. 169-80.

Harris, R.I.D. (1988), "Technological change and regional development in the UK: Evidence from the SPRU database on innovations", *Regional Studies*, vol. 22, no. 5, pp. 361-74.

Harris, R.I.D. (1990), *Regional Economic Policy in Northern Ireland 1945-1988*, Avebury, Aldershot.

Hitchens, D.M.W.N. and O'Farrell, P.N. (1987), "The Comparative Performance of Small Manufacturing Firms in Northern Ireland and South East England", *Regional Studies*, vol. 21, no. 6, pp. 543-54.

Hitchens, D.M.W.N. and O'Farrell, P.N. (1988a), "The Comparative Performance of Small Manufacturing Firms located in South Wales and Northern Ireland", *Omega*, vol. 16, no. 5, pp. 429-38.

Hitchens, D.M.W.N. and O'Farrell, P.N. (1988b), "The Comparative Performance of Small Manufacturing Firms located in the Mid-West of Ireland and Northern Ireland", *Economic and Social Review*, vol. 19, no. 3, pp. 177-98.

Hitchens, D.M.W.N., Wagner, K. and Birnie, J.E. (1990), *Closing the Productivity Gap: A Comparison of Northern Ireland, The Republic of Ireland, Britain and West Germany*, Avebury, Aldershot.

Hitchens, D.M.W.N., Wagner, K. and Birnie, J.E. (1991), "Improving productivity through international exchange visits", *Omega International Journal of Management Science*, vol. 19, no. 5, pp. 361-68.

Hughes, G. (1991), "Are the costs of cleaning up eastern Europe exaggerated? Economic reform and the environment", *Oxford Review of Economic Policy*, vol. 7, no. 4, pp. 106-36.

Icks, A. (1992), "*Mittelstandische Unternehmen als Qualifizierungspaten*", *Schriften zur Mittelstandsforschung*, no. 49, Stuttgart.

IDB, (1990a), *Forward Strategy 1991-93*, Industrial Development Board, Belfast.

IDB, (1990b), *Forward Strategy 1991-93 Competitiveness and its Measurement*, Industrial Development Board, Belfast.

IFO, (1991), "*Konjunkturtest in den neuen Bundeslandern*", *Schnelldienst*, no. 16-17.

Institut der Deutschen Wirtschaft, (1991), "*Marketing in Ostdeutschland*", *Selbsvertrauen wachst*, no. 45.

Institut der Deutschen Wirtschaft, (1991, June 20), no. 25.

Institut der Deutschen Wirtschaft, (1991, July 11), "*Regionale Bennpunkte*".

Institut der Deutschen Wirtschaft, (1992), "*Informationsdienst des Institut der Deutschen Wirtschaft*", January 16, Koln.

Institut der Deutschen Wirtschaft, (1992, August 13), "*Auf dem falschen Feld gejagt*".

Institut für Arbeitsmarkt und Berufsforschung der Bundesanstalt für Arbeit, (1992), "*Kurzbericht*", no. 19.

Katz, E. and Ziderman, A. (1990), "Investment in general training", *The Economic Journal*, vol. 100, no. 403, pp. 1147-58.

Kinsella, R. (1991), "German economic and monetary union (GEMU) some policy implications for Ireland", *Paper to the Economic Policy Conference of the Dublin Economic Workshop*, Kenmare, October 20.

Korn, M. (1991), "One year after unification: A new Germany in a new Europe", *Paper to the Economic Policy Conference of the Dublin Economic Workshop*, Kenmare, October 20.

Lammers, K. (1990), "*Wege der Wirtschaftsforderung für die neuen Bundeslander*", *Die Weltwirtschaft*, Heft 2, pp. 98-109.

Lee, J.J. (1990), *Ireland 1912-1985: Politics and Society*, Cambridge University Press, Cambridge.

Leibenstein, H. (1966), "Allocative efficiency versus "X efficiency", *American Economic Review*, vol. 56, June, pp. 392-415.

Lenske, W. (1992), *Strukturwandel Ost. Personalentwicklung-Qualifizierung-Rahmenbedingungen wirtschaftlicher Entwicklung. Ergebnisse einer Umfrage bei ostdeutschen Unternehmen, Deutscher Institutsverlag*, Koln.

Lipschitz, L. and McDonald, D. (1990), "German unification: Economic issues", *Occasional Paper*, number 75, International Monetary Fund, Washington DC.

Mann, C.L. (1991), "Industrial restructuring in eastern-central Europe: The challenge to EC policymakers from the role of foreign investment", *American Economic Review*, vol. 81, no. 2, pp. 181-84.

Marer, P. (1981), "Economic performance and prospects in eastern Europe: Analytical summary and interpretation of results", in Eastern European Economic Assessment, *Papers submitted to the Joint Economic Committee Congress of the United States*, Washington, pp. 19-94.

McKinnon, R. (1991), *The Ordering of Financial Liberalisation: Financial Control in The Transition to The Market Economy*, Stanford University Press, Stanford.

Merkel, W. and Wahl, S. (1991), *Das Geplunderte Deutschland: Die Wirtschaftliche Entwicklung im Ostlichen Teil Deutschlands im 1948 bis 1989*, IWG, Bonn.

Moore, B., Rhodes, J., and Tyler, P. (1986), *The Effects of Government Regional Economic Policy*, Department of Trade and Industry, London.

Muellbauer, J. (1986), "Productivity and competitiveness in British manufacturing", *Oxford Review of economic policy*, vol. 2, no. 3, pp. i-xxv.

Müller, J. (1992), "Restructuring East Germany", *Paper presented to the Conference of the European Association for Research in Industrial Economics*, September 4-6, Stuttgart-Hohenheim.

Mullineux, A.W. (1992), "Privatisation in the United Kingdom and Germany: Lessons for Central and Eastern Europe", *IFG Working Paper*, no. 92-01, Department of Economics and International Finance Group, University of Birmingham, Birmingham.

NI Economic Council, (1992), "The financial services industry in Northern Ireland", *Northern Ireland Economic Council Report*, no. 91, Belfast.

Nuti, D. (1990), "Privatisation of socialist economies: general issues and the Polish case", *Paper presented to the First International Conference of the European Association for Comparative Studies*, University of Verona, September 27-29.

OECD, (1989), *Education and the Economy in a Changing Society*, Organisation of Economic Cooperation and Development, Paris.

OECD, (1991a), *Germany Economic Survey*, Organisation for Economic Cooperation and Development, Paris.

OECD, (1991b), *Services in Central and Eastern European countries*, Organisation for Economic Cooperation and Development, Paris.

OECD, (1992), *Reforming the Economies of Central and Eastern Europe*, Organisation for Economic Cooperation and Development, Paris.

O'Farrell, P.N. (1986), *Entrepreneurs and Industrial Change*, Irish Management Institute, Dublin.

O'Farrell, P.M, and Hitchens, D.M.W.N. (1989), *Small Firm Competitiveness and Performance*, Gill and Macmillan, Dublin.

O'Mahoney, M. (1992), "Productivity levels in British and German manufacturing industry", *National Institute Economic Review*, no. 139, pp. 46-63.

O'Malley, E. (1989), *Industry and Economic Development: The Challenge for the Latecomer*, Gill and Macmillan, London.

Owen, R.F. (1991), "The challenge of German unification for EC policymaking and performance", *American Economic Review*, vol. 81, no. 2, pp. 171-75.

Patel, P. and Pavitt, K. (1987), "The elements of British technological competitiveness", *National Institute Economic Review*, no. 122, pp. 72-83.

Prais, S.J. (1986), "Some international comparisons of the age of the machine stock", *Journal of Industrial Economics*, vol. XXXIV, pp. 261-87.

Prais, S.J. and Wagner, K. (1988), "Productivity and management: The training of foremen in Britain and Germany", *National Institute Economic Review*, no. 123, pp. 34-47.

Ray, G.F. (1990), "International labour costs in manufacturing", *National Institute Economic Review*, no. 132, pp. 67-71.

Ray, G. (1991), "Innovation and technology in Eastern Europe: An international comparison", *Report Series*, no. 2, National Institute of Economic and Social Research, London.

Reich, R.B. (1988), *Education and the Next Economy*, National Economic Association, Washington DC.

Report of the Industrial Policy Review Group, (1992), "A time for change: Industrial Policy for the 1990s", Stationery Office, Dublin.

Röpke, W. (1960), *A Humane Economy: The Social Framework of The Free Market*, Oswald Wolf, London.

Rostas, L. (1948), *Industrial Production, Productivity and Comparative Productivity in British and American Industries*, Cambridge University Press.

Salter, W.E.G. (1966), *Productivity and Technical Change*, Cambridge University Press, Cambridge.

Schwarz, R. (1991), *"Innovationspotentiale und Innovationshemmnisse in der DDR-Wirtschaft"*, *Discussion Paper*, FS, IV, 91-26, WZB Science Centre, Berlin.

Siebert, H. (1991a), "The integration of Germany", *European Economic Review*, no. 35, pp. 591-602.

Siebert, H. (1991b), "German unification", *Economic Policy*, no. 13, pp. 287-340.

Smith, A.D., Hitchens, D.M.W.N, and Davies, S.W. (1982), *International Industrial Productivity: A Comparison of Britain America and Germany*, Cambridge University Press, Cambridge.

Söstra, E.V. (1992), *Beschaftigungsperspektiven von Treuhandunternehmen, Bundesanstalt für Arbeit, Der Präsident*.

TEA (1991), *Management Development: A Discusssion Document*, Training and Employment Agency, Belfast.

Telesis (1982), "Review of Industrial Policy", *National Economic and Social Council Report*, no. 64, Dublin.

The Independent, (1991, February 2), "Why unity spells strength".

UBS, (1989/90), "Eastern Europe: A long way to prosperity", *International Finance*, issue 2, Union Bank of Switzerland, pp. 1-8.

UBS, (1991), "Eastern Europe: Waiting for a market", *International Finance*, issue 7, Union Bank of Switzerland, pp. 1-9.

Wyplosz, C. (1991), "Post-reform east and west: Capital accumulation and the labour mobility constraint", *Discussion Paper*, no. 538, Centre for Economic Policy Research, London.

Zemplinerova, A. (1991), "The Demonopolisation of the formerly centrally planned Economies - The Experience of Czechoslovakia", *Paper presented to the Conference of the European Association for Research in Industrial Economics*, September, Ferrara.